Dedication

For Sarah and Neave

First published in March 2011
Reprinted in paperback 2016

A catalogue record for this book is available from the British
Library

ISBN 978 1 78521 092 1

Library of Congress catalog card no. 2010934896

Published by Haynes Publishing,
Sparkford, Yeovil, Somerset BA22 7JJ, UK

Tel: 01963 440635
Int. tel: +44 1963 440635
Website: www.haynes.com

Haynes North America, Inc.,
861 Lawrence Drive, Newbury Park,
California 91320, USA

Printed in Malaysia

Photo Credits

All images courtesy of Steve Behr at Stockfile (www.Stockfile.co.uk)
except product shots on pages 15, 18 (www.madison.co.uk) and
pages 16-17, 18-19 (www.zyro.co.uk)

The publishers would like to thank the following for their help with
photography: Chris Smith, Rob Cole, Jack Meek, Oli Beckingsale,
Will Longden.

Mountain

Biking
Skills
Manual

Step-by-step guidance
from the experts

Alex Morris

Contents

2

Skills

3

Introduction

Mountain Biking has developed into one of the most diverse sports in modern history. The actual origins of MTBing, as we know it today, are uncertain, with some individuals claiming that riders were getting their off-road fix as early as the late 1800s. However, the most widely recognised and tangible evidence traces a distinct line back to the 1970s, Northern California, and the now legendary Marin County.

The bikes they chose back then weren't designed for riding off-road – they were far more suited to cruising the beaches in between surfing sessions. Classics like the Schwinn Excelsior with its balloon tyres and massive bars were the weapons of choice and it's not hard to spot the evolutionary development from that unlikeliest of bikes to even the most technically advanced machines we get to ride today.

Naturally the technology has moved on a lot in the 30-odd years since then, perhaps even more so than in other similar sports. And as a direct influence of that development, several branches have spurred off from the main trunk of MTBing. And with each improvement in technology, smaller branches still emerge to create yet more styles of MTBing.

Virtually no other sport has had such a rapid evolution, and to the same extent so much fragmentation. Through that evolution we've seen several sub-sports emerge from the same place, each with its own industries, enthusiasts and products. Riders who favour the thrill of downhill now have machines at their disposal that would put a lot of motorcycles to shame. Infinitely adjustable, reliable suspension systems, brake set-ups that can safely bring you to a halt from incredible speeds, and frames that can hold up under enormous strain whilst remaining nimble and manoeuvrable.

Riders who enjoy the challenge of riding cross-country can now do so on a bike that weighs next to nothing but has the benefit of intelligent suspension that isn't hindered by braking or pedalling.

All of these things have contributed to making MTBing one of the most exciting sports to be a part of, and all the developments have provided the opportunity to capitalise on all that amazing technology and change cycling from a relatively passive sport into one that can be enhanced by really understanding how bike handling can turn an ordinary ride into an experience that will leave you exhilarated, challenged and wanting to ride more.

The purpose of this book is to give you the tools you need to improve your riding, whether you're an absolute beginner, weekend rider or even someone with a lot of riding under their belt. We've worked alongside some of the best riders in the world to detail techniques from every aspect of MTB riding, from cross-country to the newer types of riding such as SlopeStyle and North Shore. And if you've yet to discover exactly what that kind of riding involves, then this could be the perfect introduction. As with other sports, most techniques develop from a core set of principles and it's the same with MTBing, so we'll make sure we cover those before leading you on to the more advanced skills.

Alex Morris
February 2011

The MTB A Brief History

As we briefly touched on earlier, the MTB's origins lie in the customised beach cruiser bikes that early pioneers used for blasting down dusty Californian mountainsides in the late '70s. At that time the term 'mountain bike' or MTB had yet to be coined, but the movement was quickly growing, and the direction of the modifications those riders were making to their Schwinn Excelsiors (widely regarded by the pioneers as the best cruiser for racing down mountains) were taking tangible strides towards the birth of the first dedicated mountain bike.

The Excelsior's chunky balloon tyres were a great starting point and riders hacked together basic gear set-ups using road-bike components and added motorbike bars for more steering control and strength. They weren't pretty and quickly picked up the moniker 'Klunkers', which was a fairly accurate description of their Frankenstein-esque appearance. Their braking system – generally a very underpowered hub brake – would get so hot on the way down the hill it'd need repacking after a fast run. The practice became so common that the unofficial race series that developed from the scene was aptly dubbed the 'Repack'.

Towards the end of the '70s the first proper MTB was built by one of the regular competitors in those Repack events. Joe Breeze used some of the latest road-cycling technology to produce a lightweight geared bike that was designed purely for off-road use. Other bikes began emerging soon after, with models branded up as 'MountainBikes', which was a collaboration between Gary Fisher, Charlie Kelly and Tom Ritchey. You might have noticed

⬇ **A hockey helmet and virtually no brakes. A world apart from modern downhill.**

a few of those names dotted around on various components on your own bike, as both Fisher and Ritchey went on to develop mainstream brands that were and still are massively successful.

MTBing hit the big time in the early '80s when Specialized took the custom-made bikes of the time and made their own mass-produced versions in the Far East. Suddenly the floodgates opened and new MTB companies began appearing at a phenomenal rate.

Developments in MTB technology came thick and fast from that point on. Transmissions went from road-style shift levers to bar-mounted

← **The iconic XT thumbshifter. Bringing reliable, controlled 'indexed' shifting to the masses.**

↓ **Specialized were at the forefront of bringing mass-produced mountain bikes to the market.**

↑ **One of the first dedicated mountain bikes. Many of the innovations still exist today on modern bikes.**

thumbshifters and along the way also picked up indexing (the system where a gear position is set using a predefined click). With advances in chain technology moving along swiftly, the number of gears also seemed to grow as each year passed, with systems starting out at 12 speeds and then rapidly moving on to 15, 18, 21 and 24 speeds. At various

stages throughout that time we saw big gears, small gears, gears that used oval chainrings to enhance power transfer and even a few attempts at electronic gears.

Brakes started out as hub-based systems like those on the Klunkers before them, followed by a brief dalliance with U-brakes, cam-brakes and variants of them before

↓ Innovative and iconically British, Pace Cycles went their own way with square-profile tubing and concepts that were way ahead of their time.

moving onwards and upwards to the beautifully simple but powerful cantilevered systems, and then on to the V-brake realisation of that concept. Disc brakes were always on people's minds, having seen them work so well in the motor industry, and in the mid-'90s we saw the first rudimentary systems begin to appear in both cable-actuated and hydraulic flavours. Nowadays they're almost de rigueur on any modern MTB worth its salt, with even budget bikes making use of them.

In MTB's second decade suspension was the big new thing. Several manufacturers put a basic fork into production and, although pricey, opened the door for early adopters to get a taste of what was to come. For those who couldn't afford a fork, one manufacturer offered a hinged handlebar stem with an elastomer damper that was surprisingly effective once you got over the initially strange sensation of riding it. Suspension technology went from systems with almost no travel, damped by

← Doug Bradbury helped change the face of mountain biking as we know it by bringing motorcycle technology and manufacturing techniques to the sport. The first-generation Manitou fork from 1990 helped shape the design of modern forks.

↗ MTBing has had its share of fads and fashions. Garish anodising is one that doesn't seem to go away!

8

The MTB – A Brief History

← **Suntour fell victim to market domination by Shimano, but not before sowing the seeds of the modern drivetrain – Micro Drive lead the way with compact cassettes and smaller chainrings.**

⬇ **Pro-flex championed the concept of lightweight full suspension mountain bikes.**

lumps of rubber with very little control over their behaviour, to complex air, oil and spring systems, with countless combinations of these in between. Motorcycle-style triple clamp forks appeared for downhill bikes and frames had to be rethought to cope with the stresses that came with all that extra leverage.

Mountain biking has had its fair share of trends, fashions and fads over the years too. We've ridden out the hideous period when every component of your bike had to be anodised blue or purple. We've just about

survived the phase where people were drilling and chopping off parts of their bikes to save grams of weight. And most happily of all, we're through the other side of a period no one likes to discuss much where it was deemed clever to wrap yourself in neon-coloured lycra before you went out in public.

MTB's past is colourful, fascinating and incredible in even parts, but 30 years on there's still a sense of innovation, creativity and excitement to it that you'd be hard pushed to find in any other industry or sport.

9

Bikes & Kit

MTBing has come a very long way in its relatively short life, bringing with it an entire industry made up of companies specialising in everything from hardware upgrades through to technical clothing and protection.

Like with any sport, having the right kind of kit can make an enormous difference to your experience. Of course it's possible to get out riding with the barest of essentials but if you intend to ride a lot, then you'll soon find that specialist or personally tailored equipment can genuinely enhance your riding and help you ride better too.

Here's a brief intro to the types of bikes and kit you'll need to get started and some tips on how to choose the right products for you.

← **XC trail riders tend to favour more relaxed riding kit, over traditional tight-fitting lycra, and ride all-purpose bikes.**

XC/ Trail Riding

XC bikes of old were very simple stripped-down machines designed for speed, low weight and nimble handling. Aesthetically they shared many similarities with racing road-bikes, but with a more upright riding position and slightly beefier tubing.

Modern XC bikes are able to cope with pretty tough terrain, with All Mountain bikes filling the gap between XC and Freeride for more extreme riding.

Now, XC riders have the choice of whether to run front suspension on a hardtail frame, front and rear suspension using a lightweight rear air shock or, as some riders still prefer, the pure ride of a fully rigid bike. Rear suspension systems are now suitably advanced to allow efficient pedalling and some even claim to aid climbing ability.

Frames are generally made from aluminium or butted steel, but more exotic frames are produced using materials such as titanium, carbon fibre and scandium.

Braking is predominantly handled by disc brakes, either cable-actuated or hydraulic, but some riders still favour the lighter weight and simplicity of V-brakes. An XC drivetrain generally consists of 24–27 speeds controlled using a pair of standard bar-mounted triggers or grip-shifters.

DH/Downhill

D ownhill bikes have become so advanced in recent years that bicycle designers have been joined by engineers from motorsport and the motorcycle industry to assist in the design and production of the chassis and suspension systems currently available.

Although some frames do allow for up to 12in of suspension travel at each end, the majority of manufacturers have settled on systems running to around 8in to enable a practical balance between damping and ground clearance. Frames are generally made from aluminium – a material designers can manipulate and form into a bombproof structure that's also reasonably lightweight but carbon fibre is becoming more prevalent in high-end frames.

Braking is handled by super-powerful disc braking systems, running larger than average disc rotors and beefed-up brake callipers. Whereas standard MTB disc brakes generally use one piston, some downhill systems even make use of six for ridiculous braking power.

Downhillers usually run a triple crown suspension fork with legs that extend up to the handlebar stem (much like motorbike forks). This set-up is exceptionally strong but also enables a much more direct steering response and less twisting under load.

Trials

thick sidewalls are popular.

Braking is perhaps the most important factor for trials riders to get right. For many years hydraulic rim brakes made by Magura ruled the roost, but it's now more common for riders to run powerful disc brakes instead.

Trials riders run their saddles at their lowest position for maximum clearance. Some dedicated trials bikes have an integrated saddle to save weight, and some have nothing at all.

Trials bikes have to be tough but riders need their bikes to be reasonably light to enable them to be manoeuvred as easily as possible. For this reason the majority of trials bikes are made from lightweight heat-treated aluminium.

Trials bikes started out using very similar designs to traditional XC frames. In fact many riders started their trials careers riding very small XC bikes.

Most trials riders run standard 26in wheels but a small number have started to experiment with 24in wheels as well. Tyres have to be able to handle big impacts at lower than average pressures, so large-volume tyres with

Dirt / Street

abuse and, should it break, will do so in a controlled manner. When aluminium frames fail there is very little or no warning beforehand.

A lot of BMX technology has made its way on to dirt and street bikes, and they share a lot of componentry such as stems, saddles, pedals and cranks.

Many dirt and street riders remove their gears for simplicity and to keep maintenance to a minimum, not to mention having less kit to damage. The bikes are run single-speed using either a dedicated hub or kits that can convert any cassette hub into a single-speed easily and cheaply.

Dirt-jumping and street-riding bikes are very similar in looks and functionality: small hardtail frames generally run with a suspension fork, but occasionally with a rigid fork instead.

Dirt and street frames need to be built tough, so although the frames are small and compact they generally use thicker tubing that adds quite a lot of bulk to them. Most serious dirt and street riders opt for a steel frame that can take a lot of

Freeride/Slopestyle

Freeride bikes started out as modified downhill bikes, the long-travel DH bikes being a good start in the right direction for the kind of ride that freeriders needed. Suspension was tweaked to allow for maximum impact absorption – slowing the rebound down to prevent getting bucked on landing and taking the sting out of large drops.

Modern freeride-specific bikes run slightly less suspension travel – around the 6in mark at either end, shorter back-ends, single-crown forks and often a full spread of gears too, which mean they can actually be ridden up hills as well as off them.

Frames are still generally made from aluminium, built to be abused but still light enough to throw around.

Braking is predominantly handled by disc brake systems, although most riders run standard single or dual piston set-ups rather than downhill-specific brakes.

Many freeride bikes run a single ring at the front and a standard nine-speed block at the rear. To keep the chain from slipping off the front ring, riders use a chain guide that holds it firmly on to the chainring.

4X

4X bikes are designed for sprinting, clearing double jumps and being thrown into corners at warp speed. Riders generally choose between a hardtail-style frame with a suspension fork or a short-travel fully suspended bike with around 4in of travel at either end.

Frames can be made from butted steel or aluminium, although the latter often provides the best combination of stiffness and light weight for maximum power transfer.

Braking is predominantly handled by standard disc brakes, and, like freeride bikes, 4X bikes generally run a spread of nine gears using a single ring at the front, managed by a chain guide with a regular nine-speed block at the back. This gives riders the opportunity to get a fast start in a lower gear then drop down to a faster gear once they've built up some speed. Tyres depend a lot on rider choice, but with cornering being such an important part of a race a tyre with pronounced cornering edges is going to be advantageous.

Trail

XC/Race

Helmets

Everyone knows that having the right kit for the job makes things a lot easier, and sometimes more fun too! In MTBing this is particularly true, and although the initial outlay isn't cheap if you choose good-quality kit to begin with you'll get plenty of value from your investment. If at all possible try not to scrimp on important items like helmets and shorts. You don't need to spend a fortune but cheaper kit can be uncomfortable and won't last, and in respect of helmets could potentially be a dangerous saving.

Although the Internet is a great way to shop, buying a helmet is really something you need to do at your local bike shop. Heads are notoriously different in shape and size, and one brand of helmet may not fit you well at all. Most riders find a brand that works for them and stick with it for life. To find the appropriate-sized helmet, put it on and ensure that it's not restrictive in any direction; you can fit thicker pads on most helmets to get a perfect fit, but the rule of thumb is to find one that fits comfortably but moves with your head when you twist it rather than being able to rotate. There are countless styles and designs and some have better ventilation than others. Your local bike shop will be able to help you find your perfect helmet so it's well worth spending half an hour with a clued-up staff member to get this right. The staff will be familiar with the myriad choices on offer too and will be able to point you in the right direction.

One thing to note with any cycle helmet is that the foam core construction is designed to absorb impacts by distorting and dissipating the force around its shape. When this has happened once, a second impact may just cause the helmet to crack and won't provide you with the level of protection it was designed for. So if you have a big crash and hit your head, return the helmet to your local shop and get it changed. Most of the big manufacturers have a crash replacement policy so that you get a replacement at a cheaper rate.

Full-face

Dirt/Street

15

Clothing

The old saying 'there's no such thing as bad weather, only the wrong clothes' is true for any outdoor activity, but for MTBing it rings particularly true. And in the UK we're blessed with particularly changeable weather, so choosing the right clothing for a ride can be even more tricky.

The other challenge with dressing for riding is that during a ride you'll experience constantly changing body temperatures, perhaps in a very short space of time too. You could be sweating up a climb one minute, only to reach the top and start a three-minute downhill, or a slog across an exposed field.

The best policy is to invest in some good technical basics and build yourself a layering system. Starting from the top, a base layer is essential; this tends to be close-fitting and available in long- or short-sleeved versions. The base layer traps body heat but also draws sweat away from the body, which makes riding much more comfortable.

As a mid-layer a thin fleece-type jacket is a good investment, primarily for keeping you warm when it's cooler. The mid-layer is also a good choice for general riding, especially if you pick something with a long zip

Base-layer

⬆ A separate short-liner, worn under baggy shorts, provides traditional levels of comfort without the 'roadie' look.

⬆ A technical base-layer will wick sweat from the skin and transfer it to a mid- or outer-layer where it can evaporate.

so that you can open or close it to regulate your heat.

Over the top and for lighter showers, a lightweight shell jacket works well for keeping light rain at bay and stops the wind from chilling you too much. If you're riding in particularly nasty weather a fully waterproof Gore-Tex jacket is an essential item, keeping even the most powerful downpours from drenching you. By combining, adding or removing the layers you'll have a really adaptable system, and be able to respond to changes in climate or your own temperature quickly and easily.

Shorts are a very personal choice, but being in the saddle for extended periods of time you're obviously going to want the most comfortable experience possible. Lycra race-style shorts or tights are very comfortable with a chamois or,

more commonly, faux-chamois insert. Modern shorts are amazingly cut with anatomically shaped inserts and seamless stitching to prevent any extra discomfort.

'Baggy'-style shorts have become more common in recent years, with a traditional race-style lycra short stitched inside a more casual and looser-fitting outer. These can be as comfortable and are great for riders who feel self-conscious wearing lycra in public.

Many companies now produce dedicated riding trousers too, which for really inclement weather are a great idea. Generally made from a waterproof fabric like Gore-Tex, they're a godsend when you don't want the rain to stop you riding. And are cut to make sure they don't hinder your pedalling.

Mid-layer

↑ **A mid-layer long-sleeve jersey will cover most riding eventualities, providing a balance of warmth with great ventilation, whilst keeping wind-chill at bay.**

↗ **A baggy short worn over a padded liner will provide all-day riding comfort. In cooler months look at ¾ length options for extra warmth.**

Outer-layer

→ **When it comes to jackets for cycling, fully waterproof is only half the story. Without sufficient ventilation and quality breathable fabrics you'll find you get just as wet from your own perspiration.**

Eyewear

↑ **Goggles offer increased eye protection and added security although ventilation can't match traditional glasses.**

↓ **Glasses with interchangable lenses offer protection under all light conditions, often including a clear lens for night time use.**

If you've ever suffered the debilitating and often dangerous experience of catching a lump of mud or errant insect in your eye whilst riding, you'll appreciate how important good eye protection can be.

Eyes are obviously very sensitive to impact, dirt and also wind, so it goes without saying it's worth investing in a set of glasses that provide appropriate coverage to catch mud and occasionally rocks and twigs, but also be able to withstand quite significant impacts too. A good-quality lens will also be treated so as not to mist up when getting hot in damp conditions and also have good optical properties so as not to distort the trail.

There are a vast number of brands which produce dedicated glasses for riding. You don't need to spend a fortune but try not to skimp when choosing glasses – you definitely get what you pay for with eyewear. Many brands provide a universal frame with a number of different lenses to suit different conditions, such as low light, bright sunshine or severe weather.

Downhill riders (and a lot of freeriders) run more traditional goggles that provide a wide field of vision, fantastic eye protection along with ventilation and the ability to be run over a full-face helmet. Goggles have become as advanced as regular glasses of late so try a few sets on and choose a set that works for your own needs.

Gloves

When it comes to choosing kit, gloves often get overlooked, despite the fact that in almost every crash you'll experience on a bike you'll get your hands down first, which means that naturally they'll take the brunt of your mishaps.

You don't need anything particularly special, and you certainly don't need to spend a lot of money. And the argument that gloves are uncomfortable really doesn't hold up any more, with a vast array of styles, thicknesses, cuts and shapes able to cater to just about any size or shape of hand.

Whether you choose long-fingered or short, you need to ensure you get exactly the right size or the glove will either be restrictive and painful or too large, leading to bunching and uncomfortable ridges where the fabric gathers.

Again this is one product you should probably purchase from a specialist shop, where the availability of a range of styles and sizes will give you the opportunity to find something that fits you correctly.

Footwear

The type of shoes you require will, of course, depend on your choice of pedal system. For flat pedals skateboard-style shoes are generally ideal. Although these don't offer much in the way of technical protection from the elements, they do provide the best grip and stiffness when paired with a good flat pedal. Combining these with a quality waterproof sock is a good compromise. You can, of course, buy specific riding shoes for flat pedals, but unless you feel that you need the extra stiffness or lace-protection etc these offer, then they aren't an essential purchase at all.

If you choose to run any of the common clipless-style pedal systems, you will of course require a compatible shoe on which to attach the appropriate cleat that engages with the pedal. Most systems are interchangeable, but occasionally you'll have to make some minor adjustments to the cleat recess in the shoe, using a sharp knife, to accommodate your cleat.

Clipless shoes come in a number of styles, ranging from very pared-down race shoes to hiking-boot style, with a myriad variations in between. As with purchasing a helmet, this is also something that's much easier done at a bike shop. Speak to the staff for advice on what's best for you. Some shoes are great for pedalling and terrible for walking in, some do the opposite. And, like helmets, different brands suit different feet, so try a few on before making your purchase.

➜ **Shoes for clipless pedals tend to have quite stiff soles to aid power transfer, but many suffer from clogging around the cleat recess in muddy conditions.**

⬇ **The soles may look smooth but skate-style shoes offer tremendous levels of grip on flat pedals.**

19

Tools & Spares

A basic toolkit is essential for every rider – even if you tend to ride in a group, being stuck on an unrideable bike in the middle of nowhere isn't much fun and can even be dangerous in more remote areas. A decent multi-tool can get you out of most situations as long as it has a spread of all the common Allen key sizes, a chain tool, cross-head and slot-head screwdrivers and a torx key if you run discs. A decent multi-tool isn't cheap, but don't be tempted to scrimp on such an important item. Halfway up a mountain with a broken bike is the last place you want to round off a bolt or snap a tool for the sake of a few extra pounds. However, although these tools can offer an amazing array of features don't get blinded by functionality you won't need. Also bear in mind that although multi-tools are great in an emergency, for day-to-day use they're quite fiddly and awkward to use.

Naturally you'll also need at least one spare tube, some tyre levers and a method to re-inflate your tyres after a flat. There are countless options involving compressed air canisters, but for reliability opt for a good mini-pump. These pumps are surprisingly effective, take up very little space in your pack and can even be frame-mounted if you prefer.

Depending on what system your chain uses, make sure you have a joining pin or connecting link with you too, so that if your chain snaps you can take out the damaged link or links and rejoin it, even if you end up with a more limited spread of gears. A gear cable inner is also a good idea for longer rides, but a well-maintained bike shouldn't suffer cable failure under normal circumstances.

←↑↓ **A saddle pack with a mini-pump, a spare tube and puncture kit and a multi-tool will cover most situations.**

STORAGE

You'll always need to carry some kit with you when you're riding. Depending on how long you intend to be out, how much kit you need to carry and what kind of riding you're doing will dictate what's best for you. Backpacks aren't ideal as they get sweaty and can be very restrictive, although some smaller, bike-specific packs can be useful on more epic rides. Seat packs are usually sufficient for most rides. Keep a spare tube, a basic tool kit and a snack in there for emergencies.

COMMUNICATIONS

It may seem like a strange thing to consider when heading out on a ride, but we've grown to take mobile communications for granted. MTBing can be a risky pastime and the very nature of the sport means that you'll be riding in areas that can be remote and inaccessible. If you get into trouble with a mechanical problem, or if you or a riding buddy have an accident, being able to get in touch with civilisation could literally be a life or death scenario.

Always ensure you have a fully charged mobile phone with you at all times. If you're riding in a group then you don't all need one, but it's prudent to keep at least a couple with the group. Also make sure you let someone know where you're headed before you set off, so that if you don't make it back they can alert the police or mountain rescue to come after you.

If you do ride regularly in a group it may also be worth investing in a set of walkie-talkies. These don't rely on a mobile signal and allow groups of riders to communicate easily if they happen to get separated.

⬇ Some new phones include GPS. The mapping may not work off road, but it'll give you co-ordinates if you get lost or need to call for help.

⬆ Hydration packs satisfy the need for water and can carry a lot of additional kit.

21

Seasonal Kit

SUMMER

Summer is a great time for riding. Dry trails ride faster and smoother and you'll be able to head out with just shorts and a jersey and enjoy riding unencumbered by layers of clothing and boggy trails.

Unlike winter riding, there isn't a great deal of specific kit you can benefit from – in fact the opposite is true, as you can strip down your bike to basics and remove any mudguards, heavy tyres and waterproofing kit you might have installed. The one area you can really capitalise on during the summer months is tyre choice. With dry and dusty trails you don't need massive chunky treads to get decent traction. You can run pared-down or even semi-slick tyres at higher pressures, which means your bike will roll faster for less effort, which enhances your bike's handling immensely through singletrack (narrow trails only wide enough for one rider) and on fireroads (fast and wide forestry trails) – not to mention the weight saving that you'll get from losing all that extra rubber. Bear in mind, though, that British summertime is notoriously changeable, so only run summer tyres if you're sure of a decent run of dry weather. Summer tyres in wet conditions are a horrible combination.

← **Ditch your bike's winter wardrobe and make the most of the dry trails.**

↓ **Semi-slick tyres can transform your bike on dry trails. You'll be amazed at the speed boost they bring.**

WINTER

Winter seems to take up the larger part of the year somehow, but manufacturers have managed to stay ahead of the game with some clever and innovative products to keep you riding even when the weather is determined to spoil your fun.

The biggest and most valuable addition you can make to your bike during winter is decent tyres. There are two things to consider for winter tyres: how the tyres actually hook up in the mud, and how well they clear mud once they're covered in the stuff. Achieving the balance between the two has been something of a holy grail for tyre manufacturers, but the choice of rubber for winter riding has now developed to the point where you can pick a set of tyres to suit the exact type of mud you ride in. For very wet, loose mud you might want something with a more spiky profile that cuts through the muck to find grip below the surface, while for thicker, sticky mud you'll want something with wide-spaced blocks that can hook up well but still lose any build-up once you get rolling again.

Your best bet is to talk to local riders and shop staff to see what other riders are using on your local trails. You'll often see the same tyres being used by lots of riders on the same trails for a very good reason.

Mudguards have a slightly geeky reputation, but there are now plenty of guards that don't make you look like the local vicar out for a spin and also manage to keep the majority of muck where it belongs. For the bare minimum a downtube-

↙ Mudguards aren't the clunky ugly products they used to be. Modern mud protection is stylish and easy to fit.

↑ You'll be glad of winter proofing both your body and your bike when the trails get soggy.

headtube. Running for about a foot along your downtube, it will prevent the majority of water and mud getting thrown up at you from the front tyre. Generally made of injection-moulded plastic these guards are innocuous enough to be left on throughout the year, but it's only when you ride without one that you realise just how valuable they are.

If getting blasted in the face from your front tyre isn't much fun then it's almost as unpleasant getting a constant stream of wet mud up your back from the rear tyre. A lightweight seat-tube-mounted guard will cure that problem in a few minutes and is so easy to install that you can whip it on and off on a per-ride basis.

Bearings take a lot of abuse during winter months despite the fact that these days the majority of components make use of so-called sealed bearings (where the bearing is held in a self-contained unit and covered by a rubber seal). Sealed bearings can vary massively in quality, and cheap bearings don't last long in very wet weather. You can help protect them by coating them in waterproof grease during

mounted guard is a godsend for winter riding. One of the biggest problems of riding in the slop is wet mud being flung into your face from your front tyre. The downtube guard attaches very simply using either rubber ties or Allen-key bolts if your frame has the mounting holes just behind the

⬆ **Make sure to carefully clean your bike and its components after a muddy ride to keep things running smoothly.**

⬐ **Speak to local riders or shop staff and see what type of rubber works best for your trails.**

➔ **With a few minor modifications you can ride in pretty much any weather – even snow!**

winter months, and when you come to clean your bike after a ride avoid aiming the hose or jet washer directly at any bearing.

Pay particular attention to headset, bottom brackets and suspension pivots. You can also purchase neoprene covers for your headset bearings, which keep most of the muck out.

Replacing sealed bearings isn't as painful as the old cup and cone systems, which used loose bearings that always went everywhere any time you had to replace or service them. You can get replacements for most components from your local bike shop or even a local bearings supplier, who may have compatible items for marine or industrial use.

Finally, braking in the winter months can be problematic. Rim brakes and wet weather don't make a good combination, and even the most powerful V-brakes will be next to useless in the rain. The solution is to upgrade

to hydraulic disc brakes. Cable-operated disc brakes have improved vastly in recent years but still suffer the problems associated with cable-operated brakes, that when mud and grit infiltrates the cable the operation can become stiff and even seize if left unmaintained. Hydraulic discs have no cable to seize, the sealed nature of their construction means that no matter what's going on outside the fluid will always flow smoothly through the system.

Disc brakes dissipate water much better, and being further away from the ground means that the braking surface isn't constantly being covered in water. A decent disc brake will operate almost as well in the wet as in the dry. Bear in mind, though, that heavy braking in muddy conditions can cause disc pads to wear quickly, so keep an eye on your pads during the winter months.

Health & First Aid

Aid

MTBing is a very physical sport, and to get the most out of your riding you need to have at least a reasonable level of fitness and strength to be able to control the bike effectively and to be able to ride at quite high intensity for an extended period of time.

That isn't to say you need to be a slave to the gym to really enjoy MTBing but building your fitness will pay dividends for your riding and allow you to ride for longer and recover more quickly too.

In this chapter we'll take you through the basics of training advice and also help you understand how nutrition can play an essential part in sustaining your energy for riding at your best over long periods of time.

We'll also take a look at basic first aid to help you look after yourself or your riding buddies should you have an accident on the trail. It goes without saying that these tips are far from exhaustive so we'd always recommend taking a proper First Aiders' course – you could save someone's life.

◀ **Be prepared for when things go wrong – MTBing can be a dangerous pastime so make sure you know some basic first aid.**

Health & First Aid  **27**

Nutrition

↑ Keep your energy up by making sure you eat properly whilst riding.

Keeping your body fuelled for any exercise is really important, but MTBing can have some special requirements depending on what kind of riding you do.

XC and endurance riders need to make sure they're well fuelled with slow-release energy to ensure that they have what they need to keep riding for extended periods of time. Food rich in carbohydrates leading up to your ride is just what you need, as carbs burn slowly, giving you a steady release of energy. Load up with a big bowl of pasta the night before a big ride and you'll be able to keep going with smaller snacks all day.

For riding that's more reliant on short bursts of energy you need food that your body can process quickly to give you an instant burst. This can be as simple as a sugary snack or chocolate bar or a tailor-made energy bar or drink.

Most importantly of all, though, hydration is key to maintaining energy throughout a ride. A famous brand of hydration pack used to run the tagline 'by the time you are thirsty, you are already dehydrated', which sounds dramatic but is essentially true. During any exercise your muscles generate heat, which raises your core body temperature. Your body then reacts to cool you down by moving the heat from your muscles into your blood, and then increases bloodflow to the skin to help that heat escape. At the same time you'll be generating sweat, which evaporates off your skin as it attempts to cool you down. Naturally as this happens you're losing fluid, which you have to replace somehow.

How you do that is up to the individual, but whether you use a bottle mounted on your bike or a hydration pack (a small backpack containing a bladder full of liquid with a hose to drink from) you need to ensure that you drink small amounts regularly to keep your fluid levels up. Try to get into the habit of having a small sip at every opportunity – if you have to stop to go through a gate or check your bearings, for example.

Always make sure you carry some kind of energy food with you on every ride. Many a rider has been caught out by a sudden energy crash – known as 'bonking'. Carry some energy gels (a concentrated version of an energy drink), a banana, some energy bars or a handful of dry fruit. In the States it's common for riders to make their own 'trailmix', which is an easy-to-carry mixture of dried fruit, nuts and small chocolates like M&Ms. This is tasty, lightweight, and provides all the nutrients you need to keep on riding.

Training & Fitness

Unless you want to ride competitively, no specific training is required to get into riding mountain bikes. A basic level of fitness is needed to be able to ride for any distance, but of course this can be developed over time.

You can build your stamina slowly over several rides, by increasing the length of your ride incrementally and aiming to push yourself a little further each time. If you have a favourite loop, start off with one circuit, then build up to a second lap and perhaps even more. If you know the loop well you can concentrate on hitting certain sections harder or saving your legs for later in the ride. After just a few rides you'll already be able to feel a significant difference in how hard and far you can ride.

Mountain biking also requires a decent amount of strength to really make the most of your riding. It's not just your legs that take a beating either – beginner riders always comment on how much their hands and forearms hurt following a long downhill. Your arms won't be used to taking a pummelling like that, and your forearms can suffer from 'pump', where the muscles are tensed for longer than they're used to and almost cramp up. If you experience this, stop for a while, relax your arms, open and close your fingers and the pump will fade.

Your torso will also begin to use muscles you probably haven't used before. As you negotiate through a winding singletrack or throw your bike into fast downhill turns your trunk will be working hard to correct your balance as you hit sections of uneven trail. So not only is mountain biking great fun, it's one of the best workouts you can have too.

Beyond improving your fitness, your riding will improve vastly if you can develop your riding skills to allow you to push yourself further on the trails. You can refer to the fundamentals section of this book for some of the most important skills to develop. Obviously the best place to work on these techniques is out on the trails, but not everyone has the luxury of being close enough to their trails to make this possible. The most important thing of all is to spend as much time on the bike as possible, even if that's riding around the car park of your local supermarket. Gaining confidence in how your bike reacts to different circumstances will pay dividends when you get back to the trails. You should practise moving the bike underneath you, shifting your weight around, reacting to hard braking and fast turns. Being comfortable throwing the bike around and knowing how it reacts will help your riding enormously.

⬆ **Build your fitness by riding familiar trails regularly and pushing yourself harder each ride.**

First Aid

Know your A, B, Cs
Airway, Breathing, Circulation

Occasionally things do go wrong and riders can and do get injured. Consequently you should have a basic understanding of fundamental first aid, to make sure you can look after someone with an injury until they can be attended to by a professional.

Upon approaching an injured rider you should conduct a primary survey.

Are you or the casualty in any danger? If you have not already done so, make the situation safe and then assess the casualty.

If the casualty appears unconscious check this by shouting 'Can you hear me?', 'Open your eyes' and gently shaking their shoulders.

If there is a response, and if there is no further danger, leave the casualty in the position found and summon help if needed. Treat any condition found and monitor vital signs – level of response, pulse and breathing. Continue monitoring the casualty

← **You or your riding buddies will have a crash at some point. Make sure you have a basic understanding of first aid but always call for medical help if you're unsure what to do.**

either until help arrives or they recover.

If there is no response, shout for help. If possible, leave the casualty in the position found and open the airway. If this is not possible, turn the casualty on to their back and open the airway.

Open the airway by placing one hand on the casualty's forehead and gently tilting the head back, then lift the chin using two fingers only. This will move the casualty's tongue away from the back of the mouth.

Listed overleaf are some of the most common injuries sustained by mountain bikers and how to deal with them on the trail. Naturally any serious injury should be referred to the local hospital's Accident & Emergency department, and if the rider isn't able to get there under their own steam you should call 999 at the earliest opportunity and request an ambulance.

31

CARDIOPULMONARY RESUSCITATION (CPR)

- If the casualty is unconscious, check their airway is open and clear – tilt their head back and lift their chin to open the airway.
- Dial 999 (or 112) as soon as you know the casualty is not breathing – then immediately start chest compressions.
- Place one hand on the centre of their chest. Place the heel of your other hand on top of the first and interlock your fingers, keeping your fingers off their ribs.
- Lean directly over their chest and press down vertically about 5–6cm. Release the pressure, but don't remove your hands.
- Repeat compressions 30 times, at a rate of 100–120 per minute, then follow with two rescue breaths.
- To perform a rescue breath ensure the airway is open, pinch their nose closed. Take a deep breath and seal your lips around the casualty's mouth. Blow into the mouth until the chest rises. Remove your mouth and allow the chest to fall. Repeat for second rescue breath.
- Repeat the combination of 30 compressions followed by two rescue breaths. Do not stop unless emergency help arrives and takes over or the casualty resumes breathing normally on their own.

SERIOUS OR DEEP WOUND

- Apply firm (but not heavy) direct pressure over a bleeding wound with a sterile bandage or clean cloth.
- Whilst maintaining steady pressure on the wound, elevate the affected part of the body above the heart if possible. (If you suspect a limb may be broken, do not move it.)
- If blood soaks through a bandage, do not remove it. Apply additional clean bandages on top of the soaked one.
- If possible, rinse the wound with tap water. Do not cleanse with soap or apply antiseptic to a deep wound. This could damage healthy tissue that is exposed due to the injury.
- Evaluate the wound to determine whether emergency medical care should be sought.
- If the wound is still bleeding after five minutes of steady pressure, seek medical care immediately.

← **Ensure that you or the casualty are in no further danger.**

→ **If the situation demands it, call 999 and request an ambulance.**

↓ **Make sure your casualty is comfortable.**

UNCONSCIOUS RIDER

■ Immediately call 999 and request an ambulance.

■ Check the person's airway, breathing and pulse frequently. If necessary, begin CPR.

■ If you think there is potential for a spinal injury, leave the person as you found them (as long as breathing continues). If the person vomits, roll the entire body at one time to the side. Support the neck and back to keep head and body in the same position while you roll.

■ Keep the person warm until medical help arrives.

■ Give them something sweet to eat or drink when consciousness returns.

BROKEN BONE

■ A broken bone is always serious enough to warrant calling an ambulance. Take these actions immediately whilst waiting for medical help:

■ Stop any bleeding. Apply pressure to any wound with a sterile bandage, a clean cloth or a clean piece of clothing.

■ Immobilise the injured area. Do not try to realign the bone.

■ Treat for shock. If the person feels faint or is breathing in short, rapid breaths, lay them down with the head slightly lower than the trunk and, if possible, elevate the legs.

DISLOCATION

■ Call an ambulance immediately for assistance.

■ Do not move the joint. Until you receive help, aim to splint the affected joint into its fixed position. Do not try to move a dislocated joint or force it back into place. This can damage the joint and its surrounding muscles, ligaments, nerves or blood vessels.

■ Aim to keep the rider as comfortable as possible, supporting the limb using rolled up clothing if possible.

Fundamental Skills

A lot of beginners (and some more experienced riders too) take basic bike-handling skills for granted. However, as these core skills will be what defines the rest of your riding it's a really good idea to ensure that you have all of these fundamentals under your belt before you begin to even think about taking your riding further. As we can all remember from those wobbly first efforts at riding as a kid, once you've mastered the basic concepts of pedalling and balance, riding a bike is actually pretty easy.

And that's where a lot of the problems lie when you try to explain to a new rider that although they can indeed ride a bike, they can't actually ride a bike all that well.

I always use the metaphor of an aeroplane for this example. A bad rider is simply a passenger on their bike, a good rider is a pilot. Riding a bike can be a very passive experience – it takes virtually no skill or effort to maintain progress along flat ground on a bike. But once you throw almost untold unpredictable variables into that scenario, like mud, roots, cambers or drops, then being passive will only end in disaster.

The point I'm making is that although you can ride a bike, understanding the best way to handle even the most innocuous scenarios will automatically make you a better rider.

The Basics

step 2

Just riding along on a bike is about as straightforward a technique as you could imagine, right? Well if most of your riding is on pancake-flat ground with no change of terrain or surface, and you never have to turn the bike, then you'd be spot on. Trouble is, most MTB trails tend not to share too many of those particular characteristics.

Bad riders stick out like a sore thumb. And when I say bad riders I don't always mean new riders either. The first thing you'll notice is their appalling posture and position on the bike. Bolt upright, saddle at the wrong height with their knees poking out like wing mirrors. They'll be weaving about oblivious to what's going on around them and have no idea what the trail ahead holds in store or how to react to it. That's generally because they don't react at all, but instead plough through regardless and assume they'll stay upright. They'll either be in the small ring, spinning the cranks furiously and not getting anywhere, or giving themselves a hernia pushing the biggest gear they have – it's never anywhere in between. You wonder how these people get any pleasure out of riding and, frankly, how more of them don't end up in A&E with a handlebar up their nose. Luckily you can avoid such ritual humiliation by following these simple tips.

step 3

step 4

1 Get comfortable (and used to) frequently changing from a seated to a standing position. Stay loose and keep your weight centred over the bike with elbows and knees bent so that the bike can move underneath you.

2 On open trails take the opportunity to use the wide field of vision to make regular checks on the distant trail ahead of you. Pick a spot about ten feet In front of the bike to look out for obstacles and terrain shifts.

3 Find a gear that you can spin comfortably whilst making good progress over the particular terrain you're riding. Spin the cranks smoothly. Jerky, stomping strokes sap energy and mean you're not in control.

4 Efficient braking will ensure that you ride as smoothly as possible. Aim to keep and use as much of your momentum as possible. Don't stab at the brakes, which will throw your weight forward and upset your balance. Scrub your speed gradually by dragging both brakes simultaneously.

Picking Lines

Having the ability to be able to evaluate and pick lines is one of the techniques that elevates a beginner rider to intermediate status. A beginner couldn't spot a line if it wandered up to them wearing an 'I'm a line' T-shirt and hat. To them, the idea that there could be more than one way to get through a section of trail is a concept ranking alongside flying cars and time travel. OK, I think you get the idea – they don't know about lines.

Learning to pick lines is not as straightforward as it sounds, though. The better a rider gets, the more lines are opened up to them. Really experienced riders will spot a way through a section that will have you gawping in utter bewilderment at how on earth they even found that line, let alone blast through it at warp factor five. Getting to be good at choosing lines only comes with confidence. Once you have confidence in your skills, confidence in your equipment, and confidence in how your bike reacts over different types of terrain, the ability to choose new, smoother and faster lines will come.

step 1

step 2

step 3

step 4

1 For maximum control of the bike through shifts in your bodyweight you need to be standing. Keep your weight bias slightly towards the rear of the bike so you can get clear of the saddle if you need to.

2 Riding tight trails when picking lines is most important, so your field of vision needs to be much tighter than normal. You don't want to be focused on the front tyre but should pick a spot a couple of feet in front so that you can identify the line you want and stick to it.

3 Managing your speed is essential to being able to get through a line you've chosen. Too fast and you'll be out of control. Too slow and you may not have the momentum to get you through. Technical lines should be coasted through (no pedalling) with your pedals level, which also helps prevent clipping on rocks or branches.

4 Always do your hard braking before entering any technical section. If you need to scrub speed make sure it's done before so that you're not upsetting your balance mid-line. If you need to slow down more during the technical section avoid too much front brake, which can cause the front to wash out or slip.

3: Climbing

MTBing may have its roots in blasting down hills but you have to earn your fun with a bit of hard work to get to the top. The most taxing of all climbs is the long slow slog. Any ride worth doing will inevitably have at least one of these, and you can either learn to love them or have every ride ruined by the prospect of 30 minutes' hard grind.

The biggest hurdle for most riders is the psychological one. Let's be honest, making your way up a seemingly unending climb isn't ever going to be like a trip to Alton Towers; that steady monotonous grind where the top is always 'just around the next bend'. You're spinning away getting nowhere fast and everyone's too caught up in that breathing lark to shoot the breeze about who's doing what to who and with what in EastEnders. The trick is to think positive, use that time to check out what's around you, soak up the scenery and enjoy being on your bike. Ignore the burning lungs, aching muscles and sweat pouring down your face – and just think, the top is only just around the next bend.

step 1

1 You're in for the long haul so get as comfy as possible. Ensure your saddle is set to the appropriate height and aim to centre your weight over the bike so you can drive the pedals as efficiently as possible.

2 The majority of long slow climbs tend not to be too technical so you don't need to watch the immediate trail all that intently. Fixing your gaze on the top of the hill is one sure-fire way of demoralising yourself at the bottom of a big climb. Instead just relax, check out what's around you and enjoy the ride.

3 Finding the right gearing and speed for a long climb is one of the hardest techniques to learn. It's tempting to just stick the bike in the lowest gear and grind away until you get to the top. The trouble is, should the trail get steeper or the terrain more taxing you've got nothing left to spare. Aim to spin the cranks at about 80–100rpm for a good compromise over speed and progress. Some bike computers can show you this or you can count in your head to get a rough idea.

4 You might wonder what the hell would you want with your brakes on a big climb. Well, if you're pedalling up eight miles of blacktop with nothing but roadkill to avoid, then you may have a point. But out on the trails you'll always need to be able to control your bike or avoid trouble, whether you're riding along the flat or stomping up a huge hill. It's always good practice to keep at least one finger covering your brakes.

step
4

step
3

step
2

41

Climbing

step
1

step
2

4: Drop Offs

This kind of drop is probably the most common, and although it's a beginners' technique I've seen more riders eating dirt after falling foul of a simple drop than on much larger, scarier drops. The problem lies with figuring out exactly how to tackle the terrain and choosing the appropriate technique for handling it. If you have the luxury of being able to stop and check out the drop first to see what your options are, then you should definitely use that opportunity. Riding something blind is always a recipe for disaster and midway down a near vertical chute is not the best time to figure out that your chainring is going to bury itself in the lip and there's a greased-up root-fest just waiting to throw you off.

If you can roll off the drop without your chainring fouling the edge of it then you stand a good chance of riding out of the drop cleanly just by hanging off the back of the bike. If your chainring fouls the edge, however, you may need to look at the advanced technique later on and launch off it to make the drop safely. As a rule of thumb anything much over a foot high and vertical is much easier to launch yourself off rather than trying to roll it.

step 4

step 3

1   Get off the saddle and move your bodyweight as far over the back wheel as possible. This ensures your centre of gravity is working as best it can to counteract the steepness of the drop.

2   Keep your eyes locked just ahead of the front wheel. You need to be aware of what's coming up so that you can react to it by shifting your weight or adjusting your speed by dabbing or releasing the brakes.

3   For drops like this you need to scrub your speed before you get to the edge. If you're going too fast, no amount of hanging off the back will be enough to counteract the extra force generated from taking the drop fast. As you roll the drop stay slow and in control.

4   Do your heavy braking before entering the drop. On the drop itself you need to maximise control. Locked wheels are useless for controlling a bike so avoid skidding at all costs. Brake evenly with a slight bias towards your front brake and feather your braking to avoid locking up.

43

Drop Offs

5: Cornering

step
2

step
1

Most people struggle with cornering when they first start out riding. A lot of the initial concern comes from a natural fear that the bike may lose traction and the tyres won't maintain grip through the bend. Getting to know the limits of your tyres, what different degrees of traction feel like, and then developing an understanding of the basic mechanics of cornering will all help to assuage that fear. As with any other situation where you need to get round a bend, whether you're in a car, on a motorcycle or on your bike, the obvious thing to do is to make the bend as smooth as possible. The tighter a bend is, the harder it is to ride it fast, so to counteract that you enter the corner as far away from the inside edge as you can and carve a smooth arc through it, hitting the apex (the middle of the bend) and exiting wide, back on the outer edge again, effectively making the bend much more gradual.

step 3

step 4

1 For bumpier trails, standing is preferable so that the bike can move around over the lumps. Otherwise staying seated is fine. Stay centred over the front and rear wheels but load your weight on the outside pedal for more grip. Get your cranks at a six o'clock position with the inside pedal at the top for clearance.

2 For the majority of corners, once you've scoped the line you want to take you should pick a spot on the exit of the corner and focus on that. This helps you stick to your line and commit to the bend without getting distracted midway through the turn.

3 Get your cornering technique dialled before attempting to hit anything fast. Find an appropriate bend and ride it a few times slowly, before building your speed up as you gain confidence. For slower, tighter corners turning with your bars is OK. For faster corners see below.

4 You should aim to avoid braking inside a corner. If you're rolling into the bend too fast do all your braking before you enter the turn. If you dab the brakes through a corner you can lose traction and slide out, or get forced upright, which will send you offline and off the trail.

Getting Quicker

1 If you want to be fast you need to be fully in charge of the bike. Set yourself up in the attack position with your backside just behind the saddle, arms and legs bent, ready to react to the trail ahead.

2 Check the trail out as far ahead as you can, to prepare for sudden changes or obstacles. Avoid watching what the front wheel is doing at all costs – you need to know what's coming up, not what's happening now.

3 Maximise your speed by picking the smoothest, cleanest line down the hill. Avoid nasty, speed-scrubbing obstacles and make the most of the flat sections by getting some pedalling in. Make sure you're running the highest gear you can push so that you don't spin out, which can throw your balance off.

4 Keep your braking conservative to maximise your speed. Aim to keep your speed in check by dragging the brakes rather than having to panic and slam them on when you lose control. The front brake is most effective at slowing you quickly if the trail isn't too slippery. Avoid locking up at all costs – locked wheels are unpredictable at best and dangerous at worst.

step 3

step 4

Smooth and confident riders are always going to be faster on the downhills than someone who's tense and nervous. There's only one way to build this confidence and that's riding as often as you can and getting your technique dialled to the point that you don't even think about it any more. For example, if you come across a rooty section flat out you'll simply check your speed a bit, spot your line through it and blast through without even being aware of the process. Every aspect of that potentially difficult section will be handled almost automatically, your brain and body working together to make small adjustments and get you through in one piece.

7: Downhill Basics

step
1

The fundamentals of downhill technique are more to do with being comfortable and balanced on the bike than anything else. Your body position – and, to a certain extent, state of mind – dictate exactly how you react to the trail ahead. You need to be as relaxed as you can be and ready to adapt in a calm and controlled way to whatever the trail throws at you. If you're stiff and tense you get thrown off line, get bucked into the air by roots and rocks and have zero control over what the bike is doing. A panicked rider is a scary thing to watch – if you've ever seen a rodeo you'll have a pretty good idea what one looks like. Hanging on for dear life is not the way to ride downhill.

step 3

step 2

step 4

1 Set your body position with a slight bias towards the rear of the bike. Keep your arms and legs bent so they can act as natural suspension and you can react to sudden changes in the terrain ahead.

2 You'll be travelling faster than on a regular flat trail so obviously you need to be aware sooner than you would normally of any imminent changes in the terrain, or to spot any obstacles looming ahead. Pick a spot a good 10–12 feet off the front wheel; this should give you plenty of time to react.

3 Your speed is obviously going to be a lot faster on a downhill. This means that everything happens much faster. You need to be totally focused and ready to react to the trail. Now is not the time to be pondering the meaning of life – save that for your next big climb. Top downhillers have reflexes like a panther. Be a panther. Grrr.

4 If the surface you're riding on is loose then avoid braking at all if you can and wait until the trail firms up. If it's smooth and dry you can brake later and harder and get away with it. Hard braking with a bias on the front brake will slow you down quickest, but don't overdo it or you'll be munching on mud pies.

49

Downhill Basics

8: Using Your Suspension

Technological advances over the last few years have totally changed the way we think about riding downhill fast. Suspension is now pretty much standard across all levels of MTB, whether that's just a front shock or a fully suspended set-up. Either way, the quality of the shocks has made it possible to ride over and across terrain that would have been impossible not that long ago. Rocks, roots, lumps, bumps all make blasting down hills even more exhilarating. You have to think fast, pick your lines and make the bike work hard to get the most benefit from the suspension. This has made old-school thinking on bike handling slightly redundant. Although the basics remain the same, riding a suspended bike requires a subtly different approach in order to get the best results.

step 2

step 1

50

Using Your Suspension

spension

step 4

step 3

1. The top riders make insanely fast trails look easy by making the process seem effortless. To ride like them stay loose and relaxed, centred over the bike with a slight bias towards the back if the trail is steep, arms and knees bent ready to suck up anything that comes their way. Sometimes this is known as the attack position.

2. It's a strange quirk of the human mind that on a clear trail with one dangerous obstacle on it, if you focus on that obstacle you're pretty likely to clatter into it. Don't focus on any one obstacle but rather on the exit you've picked to get through or past it.

3. Scary as it sounds, the faster you hit rough terrain the smoother you will probably find your bike rides over it. If you hit a rooty section at full tilt your bike will catch a little bit of airtime and you'll float across the top of it. Staying loose allows the bike to move around beneath you.

4. It's not a good idea to be doing any braking over rough ground as there's too much potential to hook up on an obstacle and get flipped off. Do your heavy braking before the section and, of course, cover your brakes in case you absolutely have to haul on the anchors on the bumps.

Cross-country **Cross-country Skills**

Skill

Although the roots of MTBing are firmly planted in downhill, for many riders cross-country or XC is where the majority of their riding comes from. It's fair to say that most riders out there ride some form of XC, and when MTBing went mainstream it wasn't out and out downhill machines that were flying out of the shops; it was the trusty, versatile, faithful old XC bike that truly made its mark as what most people would consider to be a mountain bike.

XC can mean different things to different people and there's plenty of snobbery inherent within the subtle sub-types of XC rider. You have your average weekend warrior, who might blast around their local forest, just having fun riding. Then you have your enduro riders, who slog for hours and hours and sometimes days pushing themselves physically and mentally. Then you have your racers, who aren't a million miles removed from their road-cycling cousins. All of whom do essentially the same thing, but with very subtle differences. And yet, once again, we see another splintered section of MTBing with its own very distinct scene, components and even fashion, to a certain extent.

But whichever version of XC you enjoy doing, the techniques you need to learn remain the same whether you're a racing snake or a pub ride hero. Here are some useful techniques to help you improve your XC riding whichever form it takes.

9: Singletrack

Singletrack

step
1

You have to be damned good to ride singletrack well. Take a track a couple of feet wide, throw in a bunch of gnarled-up roots, a few moss-covered rocks and some slippery cambers and pedal-snagging stumps, then ride it as fast as you humanly can. With trees whistling past just inches from your bars and a seriously constricted field of vision, the slightest mistake can have you face down in the dirt before you can say 'Where'd that branch come from?'

It takes years of riding to have the skills to be able to hammer singletrack and make it all flow together. You need lightning-fast reactions, the ability to pick lines on the fly as the trail changes, and the bike-handling smarts to be able to adapt to just about anything as it happens. You hear a lot of riders evangelising about singletrack riding. For many it's the ultimate test of XC bike handling. It certainly separates the men from the boys on a group ride. Railing through tight winding trails six inches from the guy in front's back tyre is a rush that you have to experience to really understand. If you need a reason to teach yourself to ride properly this has to be it.

1 Singletrack requires a lot of body English if you want to ride it hard. Your weight needs to be constantly shifting to help the bike through the tight trail. You'll be continually in and out of the saddle. Use your arms and legs as dampers and allow the bike to float beneath you.

2 With limited vision you need all the information you can get. Aim to check out what's ahead as much as possible with quick glances. Otherwise keep your eyes locked on the trail ahead approximately three to four feet beyond your front tyre. If you're following another rider, watch their body movements and aim to follow their lead.

3 We're after maximum speed through singletrack so maintaining good momentum is key. Try to run your gears in a ratio that allows you to accelerate smoothly. Be constantly ready to hit your shift triggers, to either drop or shift up a gear depending on what the trail throws at you.

4 One of the most exciting things about singletrack is that you don't know what's around the next corner. Keep this in mind and make sure you have your brakes covered. Most brakes can slow a bike as effectively with one finger as two these days, so there's no excuse not to have at least one finger on the lever at all times.

Singletrack

10: The Short Sharp Shock

step 1

As nerdy as it may sound the short, sharp shock is one description of a riding scenario that does exactly what it says on the tin.

The short, sharp shock climb catches nearly everyone out at some point. First of all it's steep and covered in big lumps, and then to add insult to injury they bung a few wet rocks and roots in as well. Anyone would think they didn't want you riding up it at all. Most beginners tend to do one of two things when facing one of these for the first time. They either hit it flat out and see what happens, or take a good look at it before opting to get off and push.

Let's face it, neither of these two techniques is going to get you very far, is it? So if you're struggling with getting up those evil steep sections of trail you'd better read on.

1 Get out of the saddle as early as you can. You need to really attack these climbs and be in absolute control. Stay as loose as possible, using your elbows and knees as dampers, and allow the bike to move as freely as possible underneath you to soak up the lumps and bumps.

2 Keep your eyes locked a couple of feet ahead of the front wheel. You need to be aware of every little obstacle the trail is throwing at you. Unlike heading downhill you don't have the same momentum to carry you over rocks and roots, so picking the right line is essential.

3 The keyword here is smooth. Riding over slippery rocks and roots while putting down heaps of power through the cranks is a recipe for massive loss of traction. Keep the cranks turning in smooth circles with consistent power and avoid making any sharp or sudden stabs on the cranks that will inevitably cause you to lose grip and probably cause you to slip.

4 Make sure to cover your brakes with at least one finger at all times to ensure you can make small adjustments to your speed quickly. You can often rescue a slip with a quick dab of the brake and adjustment in speed, particularly on rooty or rocky climbs.

56

The Short Sharp Shock Climb

Climb

11: Bombholes

If you're old enough to know what the Malvern Hills Classic was then one word is all it will take to conjure up a cheesy slowmo Hollywood-style flashback of riders shooting off into the bushes, or landing on their noses from ten feet up. The Bombhole. Ahh, the good old Bombhole. I think it's safe to say that no other obstacle on any course has ever claimed so much blood and skin and kept the St John's crew as busy as the final section of the Malvern Hills course. The first time I saw it I couldn't figure out what was causing the riders so much trouble. Then I rode it and found out. The trail leading into the Bombhole was smooth and very fast, then you disappeared into the deceptively whippy crater of the Bombhole and got spat out at warp speed off a natural launch ramp. For riders who weren't used to getting off the ground it caused havoc, either a mixture of sheer panic or plain inexperience meant that you were guaranteed some carnage pretty much all day long.

Bombholes are great fun to ride through and you needn't be scared of riding them fast – if you're in charge of your bike then you can do what you want with the crater, suck it up and ride through, or pump it for all it's worth for a bit of airtime.

step 1

step 2

step 3

Bombholes

step
4

1 So that you can react to sudden changes in the terrain and be ready to shift your weight around, get out of the saddle as early as possible. As you drop into the bowl of the bombhole get your weight over the back of the bike. In the base of the bombhole shift your weight forwards again to counteract the natural forces trying to spit you out of the exit.

2 Once you've dealt with the initial hurdle of getting into the bowl of the bombhole safely, your next big challenge is dealing with the steep exit and getting out again in one piece. As you're moving so fast, pick a point near the top of the exit and use that to gauge exactly when you need to start sucking up the momentum you generated from the downslope.

3 It's no fun riding bombholes slowly but you need to find a sensible balance between flat out and a speed you can actually counteract by soaking up the bike's natural desire to throw you out of the exit. Have a few dummy runs to see what you can get away with. Too fast and you'll struggle to control it, but too slow and you may not have the speed to make it out of the crater.

4 If you need to brake at all in a bombhole the best place is in the flat bottom of the bowl before you get sent up the transition towards the exit. For maximum effect drag both brakes, but with a slight bias on the front if the ground isn't too slippery.

12: Chutes

Chutes

Longer drops can be really intimidating if you're not experienced in how to ride them. Any drop over a couple of feet in length that's not quite vertical is also known as a chute. These are pretty much always best ridden rather than launched off, and as long as you keep your weight well back and stay relaxed there's nothing to be particularly nervous about.

Chutes are really good fun to ride and the gnarlier the surface, the more fun they get.

You need to be confident in your ability and comfortable on your bike before dropping into a chute the first few times. It's a good idea to be completely familiar with your bike so that you know how it handles and where to put your weight to make it do what you need it to. If you start flapping and panic midway through, that's when things start to get messy. Keep your braking controlled and whilst you're learning the techniques avoid riding on particularly loose or wet trails, as this adds a whole new dimension of complexity to the techniques. You're best learning to walk before you can run.

step 1

step 3

1 Always tackle chutes standing up on the pedals. Transfer your weight towards the back of the bike by getting behind the seat and hanging over the back tyre.

2 Don't focus too hard on what the front wheel is doing. Fix your gaze a couple of feet ahead and look out for the exit of the chute. This way you won't get hung up on the steepness of the trail and you'll use your sense of balance to naturally react to the trail beneath you.

3 Most chutes are really hard to ride fast, so make sure you get all your heavy braking done before you hit the top of the chute itself. You need to be absolutely in control of the bike before you drop in, not reacting to it as it happens.

4 You need to find a good compromise between controllable speed and not braking so hard that you lose balance. Don't lock either wheel if you can avoid it; drag both brakes but be aware of what each wheel is doing so that you can brake harder or let up if you feel the wheels starting to break traction.

step
2

step
4

13: Big Drops

It's been agreed by the council for good taste in mountain biking (CFGTIMB) that the word 'huck' should be struck from the vocabulary of all MTB riders. It should never have arrived in the first place – 'hucking' (or herking) is something perma-tanned French ski instructors called Claude talk about. Thankfully it has gone the way of purple anodising (despite an ironic comeback in 2009) – one of CFGTIMB's most successful takedown campaigns. It is no more, it never existed, it is an ex-phrase.

So big drops are now just big drops, which I think we all agree is much easier for us to swallow. If the trail you're riding drops away vertically and there's no way you can ride down it, then you have two choices: get off and climb down it or leap gracefully off it. Now that a lot of us are riding trail bikes with a few inches of travel at each end that's not such a frightening prospect as it used to be. You do, however, need to be supremely confident you know what you're doing before taking on a big drop, as the stakes are much higher in regard to injuring yourself if it all goes wrong. As always, start small and work your way up and you'll be herking just like Claude before you know it.

step 1

step 2

step 3

Big Drops

1 Stay loose on the bike with your weight set a little towards the back. Use your arms and legs like big springs to get a good pop off the edge of the drop and keep them slightly bent to soak up the landing smoothly. (For drops to flat get the back wheel down first – if the drop has a downslope aim to get the nose down and match the angle of landing as closely as possible.)

2 As you approach the lip, focus on your take-off spot so that you know exactly when to get the front wheel up. Once you're airborne locate the spot you want to land on so that you know when to brace for impact.

3 Rolling off a big drop without any momentum is a recipe for disaster, but by the same token hitting it at warp speed is equally as dangerous. You need just enough speed to clear the lip of the drop and any obstacles that may be poking out on the way down. As you get more confident you can always hot things up a bit if you want to.

4 As has already been mentioned, you don't want to be hitting drops at warp speed if you want to ride out in one piece. Make sure you do all your braking early so that you hit the edge at exactly the speed you're comfortable with. Once you've left the lip cover the rear brake in case you land with the front wheel too high, to prevent yourself looping off the back.

14: Rocky Trails

step **1**

step **2**

step **3**

Howling down a nice fast trail only to come face to face with a section that looks like a comedy enlargement of the rockery in your Nan's garden can be a pretty scary experience. Rocks are nasty, evil things that would like nothing better than to pitch you over the bars and then bounce your bike off your noggin just to rub salt into the wound.

Well that's what they want you to think anyway, those pesky lumps of … er, rock. But rocks aren't evil at all. In fact if you learn to ride them right they can be amazing fun, and not at all scary either.

1 Always hit these standing up so that you can shift your weight around and react to bumps and knocks. Rocks and big roots will buck you forwards if you hit them fast, so set your weight back just behind your saddle. Keep your pedals level to avoid clipping on errant lumps.

2 Spot your chosen line through the section and get your trajectory firmly in your mind. Once on your line keep looking towards the exit and you'll be more inclined to stick to it – even if you do take some hits.

3 Try to maintain your speed by staying smooth and loose and choosing the cleanest lines through the section. It might be fun to bounce off rocks, but clean straight lines are usually the quickest. That may still involve taking on a few big lumps but it's worth it in the end.

4 Get fully in control before you even reach the section. Scrub as much momentum as possible so that you can be in the best position to tackle the trail ahead. If the rocks/roots are wet, stay off the brakes inside the section – locking up on slippery rocks is a horrible experience. If you have to brake, modulate the power to avoid locking up.

step
4

15: Trail Obstacles

Sometimes you'll come across an obstacle on the trail that looks a lot like the big guy upstairs didn't want you riding down it. This could be a fallen tree, a big rock or even a log put there by mean-spirited walkers who think it's funny to sabotage your favourite track (oh yes, they really do).

Either way you have two choices: get off and climb over it, or strap on your happy hat and ride over it.

Obviously there are limits as to what's possible without a nice kicker ramp, but anything up to about a foot high is more than possible to conquer for an average rider.

1 Get out of the saddle with your pedals level. Pop the front wheel up at least a foot before the obstacle. With the front wheel clear of the obstacle, unweight the rear-end by popping a bunnyhop or shifting your weight towards the front. If you can clear the obstacle cleanly, aim to do so. If not, use your momentum to carry you over.

2 You should obviously have a pretty good idea what's beyond the obstacle you intend to ride over. It's not so cool to clear a big log and then disappear down a hole. Always have a recce before you attempt it. This is one time you may want to visually keep a check on the obstacle itself so that you can adjust your position accordingly.

3 You only need enough speed to either clear the obstacle with a bunnyhop, or enough momentum to drive the bike over the obstacle if you choose to just roll it. This depends entirely on the obstacle and there's only one way to find out. It will be instantly obvious whether you need to speed up or slow down on your first run, but always err on the side of slow on your initial attempts.

4 You don't need to be too concerned with braking when clearing most obstacles this way, but always keep your brakes covered just in case you get in a pickle on the way in or out of the section. Also depending on the size of the obstacle – if you don't make it over, grabbing the brakes can save you slipping back off it.

step
1

16: Fast Bends

step 2

step 3

Fast and smooth bends are great fun when you get them right. Once you have the apexing technique dialled you can apply this to much bigger, faster bends and start carving through sections of trail with some serious speed. The technique for fast bends is a delicate mixture of set-up, body position and conviction. Once you've hit that bend you need to commit to it fully, because if you panic, brake or shift your position you've pretty much blown it and you'll be struggling big-time to correct it. Stay focused, committed and confident, and if you follow the advice below you'll be cornering like you're riding on rails in no time.

1 Again, depending on the surface of the trail you can hit these types of bends seated or standing up. Keep your cranks at six o'clock and shift your weight bias into the corner as you lean into the turn. Weighting the outside pedal helps the tyres dig in hard.

2 For big sweeping bends you may not be able to see the exit if it's really long. Don't get caught out by looking at what the front wheel is doing because you'll undoubtedly wander off your line. Fix your gaze a few feet ahead until you can spot the exit – when you do, focus on that and you'll naturally hold your line.

3 Speed is what makes these corners so much fun, and you can hit these much faster than tight and technical bends. Sweeping turns are made almost entirely by leaning the bike – not by turning the bars at all. Your tyres work best when they're running on a constant edge so avoid sharp movements or shifts in position.

4 Doing any kind of braking inside a fast bend is not a particularly good idea. You need to maintain consistent contact between the ground and your tyres so anything that upsets this delicate equilibrium is a bad thing. Brake before the bend and aim to carve as smooth a line as possible.

step 4

step
1

step
2

17: Drifting Corners

rifting through bends isn't something that many of us will ever have the skill to do. It takes years of experience and bucket-loads of skill to get it right. It's amazing to watch a good rider drifting through turns at warp speed, a couple of inches either side of being totally out of control, but holding on to it by a thread and coming out the other side almost as fast as they went in. A real drift is done brakeless, you just use body English and a loose surface to get the bike into the slide. Don't get it confused with a big skid – skids are about as much use as spaghetti guitar strings and won't win you any style points at all.

step 4

step 3

1 Stay loose on the bike so that you can react to it sliding around beneath you. Keep your weight approximately centred front to back, and if you want the back to drift out more you can shift forward a little to unweight the rear end. Use your inside foot to save you if the slide goes too far.

2 You need to have a better idea about what your wheels are up to so don't fix your gaze too far off the front of the bike. Ideally you need to be checking out the exit whilst being aware of what the front wheel's up to. Things will be happening fast, so you need all the info your brain can handle.

3 It's impossible to drift through a corner slowly. You need to find the line just inside where control and disaster meet. You'll find that balance after a few runs, but expect a few big offs before you get there. Obviously the looser the surface, the easier it's going to be to get the bike sliding, so hunt around for some shale or dusty trails.

4 This one's easy. Don't brake. A proper drift is done without any influence from the brakes. If you're braking then you're skidding, not drifting. If you have to brake at all do it before the corner.

Drifting Corners 71

18: Very Rough Ground

1 Attack the section with your weight set a little towards the rear of the bike. Should you clatter into a large rock or root the bike will be less likely to flip over. If you have suspension aim to unload it before you hit the section by pumping then decompressing it. That way the suspension has most of its travel to work with over the lumps.

2 Look out for any particularly scary-looking rocks or roots on the way in, and set your line based on that information. Once your line is set, keep your eyes locked on the exit, which helps keep your line even if you're getting knocked all over the shop by the terrain.

3 As we mentioned earlier, hitting a gnarly section of rocks and roots slowly is a bad idea. Keep your wheels rolling with plenty of momentum and you'll actually find the section much easier. You have to find that speed with a few trial runs through the section.

4 Sometimes brakes can be a hindrance. You instinctively grab them when things get a bit hectic, but that's precisely the wrong thing to do over the lumps and bumps. Rolling wheels grip better, and locked rubber over (usually) slippery misshapen rocks and roots is a recipe for disaster. If you have to brake, do it in a smooth patch, or just modulate them well so that they don't lock up.

step **2**

step **3**

step **4**

When the trail you're riding gets really lumpy, whether that's a bunch of rocks or roots or just eroded dirt, that's often the point when a lot of riders feel it's time to grab a big handful of brake and ride through slowly and carefully, taking the supposed easy and safe way through.

The trouble is, that's precisely when you see a lot of riders getting out of shape and coming a cropper, losing control, and in a lot of cases taking a dive off the bike. A rolling wheel with less momentum behind it tends to stop when it meets something solid like a rock or hefty root, so you can be actually causing yourself grief by panicking and hauling on the anchors. The fast rider hits the rough sections even harder, using the lumps to help float over the rest by unweighting the bike and letting it iron out all the rough stuff beneath you. Whether you run full suspension or none at all, the technique is virtually the same: pick your line and stick to it and let the bike and your arms and legs do the hard work, sucking up the bumps.

19: Steep Downhills

Riding steep trails is one of those Marmite experiences – you either love it or hate it. For the adrenalin fans the steeps don't offer the same speed-induced rush as the flat-out fast trails, as you need to ride the steep stuff pretty slowly if you want to stay in one piece. For the technical riders out there it's a great way to test your handling skills as you snake your way down a section of trail that you couldn't walk up without crampons and a rope.

For beginners, steep stuff can be even more daunting than riding fast as it feels pretty unnatural to be rolling down something so steep. Whichever category you fit into there's no denying the satisfaction you'll get from making it down a really sheer section of trail in one piece and looking back up and wondering how the hell you did.

step 1

step 2

1 The old-school technique for riding steep trails was to hang off the back of the bike with your bum scraping the tyre. Things have moved on, brakes are more effective and bike geometry is better suited to the steep stuff. Set your position by straightening your arms out and staying low on the bike with your knees bent.

2 You'll be moving pretty slowly so keep your main focus a couple of feet ahead of the front tyre. If you watch the front tyre itself you'll lose balance. Every few feet take a peek further down the trail to check for obstacles or problems.

3 Speed is not your friend for most steep hills. If you have a clear run out, by all means let it go if you know you can control the rapid acceleration, but mainly you need to be rolling just fast enough to keep your balance.

4 Braking is the most important part of riding steeps. You need to have a good set of brakes you can trust and know you can modulate. Locked wheels are useless if you want to maintain any semblance of control. Drag the brakes evenly front and back and if you feel either wheel start to lock, relax that brake a little then reapply the force.

step 3

step
4

Freeride Skills

The term 'freeride' was borrowed from the world of snowboarding, and has caused countless arguments among riders who've found the phrase to be so vague as to create all kinds of confusion about what it actually means. In the true spirit of freeride – if you take the snowboarding concept and apply it to bikes – it would literally mean riding around a mountain, finding lines that other riders hadn't ridden and generally riding without restriction or constraint.

And in a way that's almost what the MTBing version of freeride has ended up as being. When riders began to realise that traditional trails weren't really pushing the new breed of bikes with 8in of suspension at either end and disc brakes powerful enough to stop a truck, they began looking elsewhere. Big mountain riding was a natural progression for riders who'd maybe spent their winters launching off big cliffs on their snowboards or skis. With the new big travel bikes, there was an obvious connection.

So riders began to experiment with what was possible. It wasn't too long before they were hitting drops and gaps that the skiers and snowboarders wouldn't even have looked at. Fifty-foot drops and gaps across enormous chasms were starting to look pedestrian. The term 'hucker' was coined to describe some of the (arguably) less skilful and stylish riders who literally threw themselves off anything and expected the bike to deal with the landing.

But now that riders have seemingly proved to themselves what's possible, the really big drops seem to have taken a back seat in favour of more creative and stylish routes down the mountain. And, in fact, freeriding has returned more to the original snowboard ideology that spawned it.

Many of the skills freeriders have developed over time have been as a result of the technology that enabled them in the first place. Here we'll take a look at a few of the freeride basics so that you can get started safely.

20: Ladders & Skinnies

Ladders and skinnies first came to the attention of mountain bikers when Canadian freeriders on the North Shore of Vancouver started building obstacles from fallen trees, logs and scrap wood, known as 'stunts', on their already gnarly and slippery trails – sometimes as a way to ride when the rocks and roots were too wet, and often just as a way to push their riding skills further. Once just the preserve of mad freeriders, ladders and skinnies are now starting to spring up all over XC trail centres too, as a way to spice up otherwise dull sections of trail and to provide a more technical challenge on trails that can sometimes become a little pedestrian.

Ladders and skinnies are actually distinct stunts. Ladders are, somewhat unsurprisingly, built like an actual ladder with long side sections made from fallen trees and branches, and shorter rungs that run perpendicular to the side sections and make up the riding surface. The rungs can be made from planks (often covered in chicken wire for grip), or short sections of branch for a more technical and bumpy ride. Skinnies are more commonly just made from planked sections of wood on a raised platform with a riding surface that's often not much wider than your tyres. Both require confident riding technique and good balance, but as with many of the more advanced techniques we've discussed, you can always start small and low and work your way up.

Ladders & Skinnies

1 Approach the obstacle standing up, with your pedals level to keep your weight evenly spread. Roll into the section with just enough speed to comfortably maintain your balance – balance and composure are absolutely key to riding skinnies. Ensure you hit the start of the skinny as straight as possible by choosing the cleanest possible line.

2 As you roll on to the skinny allow the bike to move freely beneath you to absorb any sudden jolts that may throw off your balance. Cover your brakes but try to avoid any sudden braking that will lose you momentum and affect your balance. Try to avoid watching your front wheel by focusing your vision on a spot two to three feet (just over a wheel's length) ahead.

3 Inevitably you'll have to pedal at some point, so make sure to use controlled but positive strokes to maintain speed, and if you feel like you're losing balance try sitting down briefly and pedalling in smooth rotations until you're able to stand back up.

4 Always be mindful of how and when the ladder ends – some roll out to flat, others have drops or gaps to contend with, so be sure to have walked the section first. If you need to compose yourself before tackling the drop or rollout, then a controlled trackstand (balancing the bike using a combination of body position and chain tension against locked brakes to make small adjustments to your balance) will buy you valuable seconds to prepare for the exit.

21: Teeter-totters & Seesaws

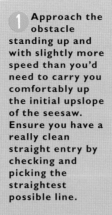

1 Approach the obstacle standing up and with slightly more speed than you'd need to carry you comfortably up the initial upslope of the seesaw. Ensure you have a really clean straight entry by checking and picking the straightest possible line.

2 Teeter-totters are usually pretty steep at both ends, so as you hit the upslope you'll get a pretty decent jolt and lose a large chunk of your speed. You need to be prepared for this and suck up as much of this impact as possible using your arms and legs whilst keeping the front wheel locked as straight as you can.

3 Occasionally you'll need to put a pedal stroke or two in if you do lose a lot of speed or the obstacle is uncommonly large. As with riding skinnies, make sure to use controlled but positive strokes to make the most out of every bit of motion.

4 As you reach the fulcrum (the point at which you have enough weight over the centre of the obstacle to cause it to tilt), dab your brakes a touch to give the see-saw a chance to start dropping before you've ridden too far on to the downslope. The aim is to get the end of the seesaw to touch the ground just before you roll off it. This takes some practice and you'll find yourself with some quite abrupt exits until you figure out timings and balance.

step **3**

step **2**

step **4**

These are essentially ladders with a raised section under the centre for the ladder to pivot on – exactly like a child's playground seesaw. For the first half of the stunt you're riding up the obstacle, then when there's enough weight past the fulcrum the ladder pivots downwards and drops to the ground so you can ride off.

Most kids probably built a basic version of this in the street when they were growing up, using a plank and a brick, but many North Shore-style teeter-totters are anything but basic and can put the rider a good few feet off the ground at the highest point. They can be great fun to ride, but a little unsettling at first as you get used to the sensation of rolling past the tipping point and feeling the ladder start to drop whilst you try and hold your balance long enough to ride out smoothly. Depending on the size of the teeter-totter you'll often find the exit to the section is blind until you start to tip past the balance point and the end of the ladder starts to drop. So as with any section on a trail that you need to ride blind, always walk it first and identify any rocks, drops or obstacles that you need to consider.

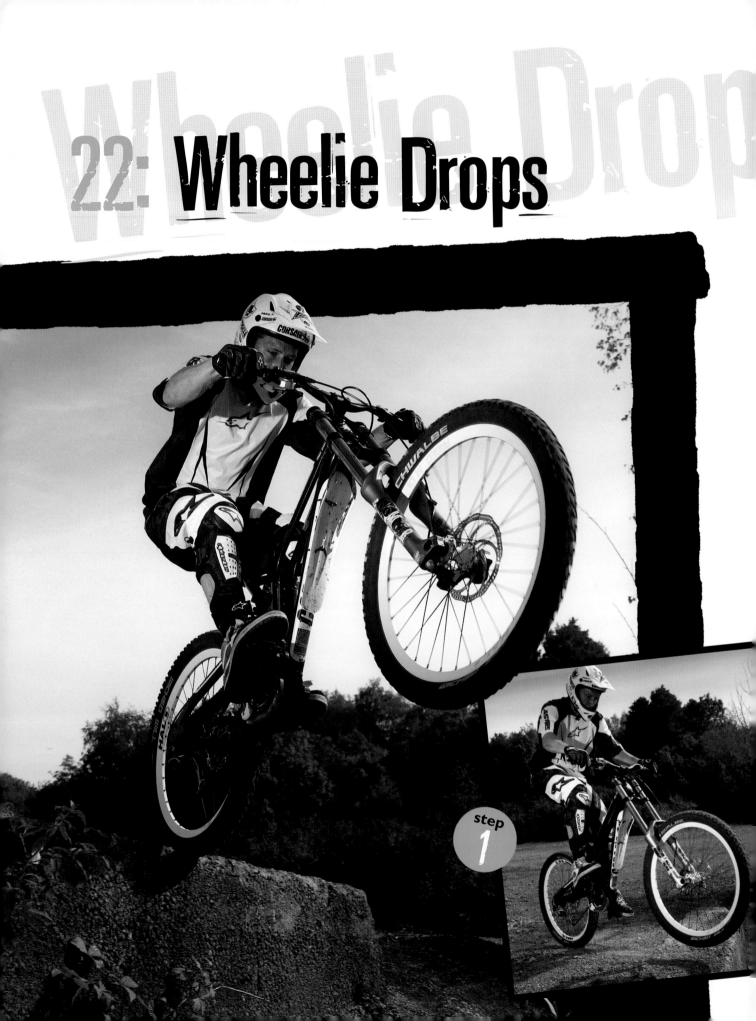

22: Wheelie Drops

step
1

In the true spirit of freeride, if the trail happens to get interrupted by a drop or large rock, the only honourable thing to do is to ride off it. Modern all-mountain bikes or freeride-specific bikes are built to take this kind of abuse, but you should perhaps exercise a little more caution on more XC-orientated bikes that weren't designed for such high impact riding.

A lot of freeriding is on steep technical trails that you need to ride at slower speeds to maintain control. As you've probably gathered, rolling straight off a drop head first is never likely to end well, and is a very common cause of front-end failures from snapped frames and occasionally forks.

You need to ensure you get a clean launch from the edge of a drop so that you can influence the position of the bike in the air. For relatively flat landings you should aim to land rear wheel first, or for sloped landings aim to match the angle of the downslope you're landing on.

Getting the front wheel up to tackle a drop without much momentum can be hard (or even impossible in certain circumstances), so a lot of riders favour the wheelie drop to launch off natural ledges or large rocks. The wheelie drop works by using torque from the drivetrain through the pedals to unweight the front end. Being able to loft the front wheel sufficiently so that you can tackle drops at really low speeds or even from a standstill is a vital skill for any freerider and opens up an enormous amount of options and trails that might not otherwise be rideable.

1 Approach the edge of the drop rolling at about walking pace, with your cranks set so that your leading foot (the foot you generally run at the front when your pedals are level) is at the 12 o'clock position. You'll be using about a quarter turn of the cranks to loft the wheel and then make sure your pedals are level for a smooth and balanced landing. As you get more confident you'll find you can set your pedal position much later. Ensure you've selected a mid-range gear that gives you enough torque to loft the wheel, but isn't too hard to push from slow speeds.

2 As the front wheel approaches the edge, drive your top foot firmly downwards and simultaneously shift your bodyweight towards the rear wheel whilst starting to unweight the front wheel with your arms. You shouldn't be relying on just your arms to get the front wheel up, the majority of this force should come from your pedals and using the torque from the drivetrain to lever the front up.

3 You'll need to tailor the amount of lift the front wheel needs based on the size of the drop. It's a pretty simple thing to fix but requires trial and error. If you find yourself looping off the back, reduce the pedal force. If you find yourself landing too front-heavy, increase it. Ensure you continue driving the pedals as you leave the drop to maintain the momentum, but aim not to push the cranks too far past horizontal or you'll find it hard to reset their position for landing.

4 Once the bike has left the edge, be sure to cover your rear brake in case you need to correct the wheelie. Beginner riders often prefer to lock the brake on in mid-air so that when the bike touches down the front end is forced down as the front pivots forwards against the locked wheel. You'll find you need to do this less as you learn how to position the bike in the air and maintain a nice uninterrupted flow through the section. Absorb the drop as you would for any other type of drop, by using your knees and elbows as dampers, and ride out.

step 2

step 3

step 4

Wheelie Drops

step
1

step
2

step
3

Ladder drops have become a standard fixture of most North Shore trail set-ups. They can be slightly daunting at first as the drops are completely sheer and you absolutely have to commit to them or you'll crash. Whereas with natural drops on trails you often have a bit of leeway, or options as to how to ride them, for ladder drops there really is just one way down.

Dependent on the ladder section that leads up to the drop you'll be carrying different amounts of speed on different drops. The two drops can be tackled using the same technique, but as you get more confident your execution will no doubt get a bit more flamboyant and you'll be able to hit the drops harder, faster and making the most of your hang time in the air.

The basic premise is similar to the wheelie drop, where your aim is to prevent the front wheel from dropping off the obstacle by lofting it off the ground just before the edge of the drop, and then positioning the bike in the air to provide the smoothest landing and exit.

As you'll have some momentum you'll use a rolling drop technique, where you use your arms, bodyweight and legs to pump the bike into rolling momentarily on its back wheel. You probably do this naturally when riding off kerbs and small drops, and you just need to exaggerate the motion and be more prepared for the greater impact, and to prevent the bike looping you off the back if you overdo it.

1 You can ride this type of drop at pretty much any speed, but you'll need at least enough momentum to carry you cleanly off the edge. Naturally, start off slowly and work your way up. Riding into the drop, preload your upper body and arms so that you can use that energy to pop the front wheel up unassisted.

2 As you approach the edge use that preloaded energy to give the bars a good heave, whilst simultaneously moving your bodyweight backwards and pumping the rear wheel forwards with your feet. You're essentially pivoting the bike on the back wheel using sheer momentum.

3 As the front wheel starts to lift, be very mindful of looping too far backwards. A small dab of the brakes can correct this and you'll get away with it. A big handful of brake will just drive the front wheel straight back down and you'll leave the drop nose-down and probably crash. Make sure you've learned how your brakes react under different conditions and how to feather rather than lock them.

4 As you leave the edge allow the bike to drop beneath you, then straighten out your legs to plant the back wheel down first. As you touch down you might want to just dab the rear brake to prevent looping off the back and force the front wheel down. Suck the landing up with your knees and elbows and ride out.

step
4

Ladder Drops

85

Dirt-jumping Skills

Skills

Since MTBs first became popular riders have always used them for dirt-jumping. Perhaps it was because the bikes were tough and easy to throw around, or perhaps riders just realised how adaptable the MTB could be. Over time not only has dirt-jumping become increasingly popular, but we now have a whole separate industry devoted entirely to MTB dirt-jumping, with national and international contests, dedicated products and a vast array of specially created dirt-jump spots all over the country.

Up until recently MTB dirt-jumping, although still very popular, was deemed to be something of an inferior version of BMX dirt-jumping. In its infancy most of the riders hadn't yet grasped many of the important tricks that the BMXers had already made standard, and the hardware available was somewhat restrictive. Now that this is no longer the case the gap between BMX dirt-jumping and MTB dirt-jumping is almost imperceptible, with MTB riders being able to pull all of the BMXers' most impressive tricks. We've even seen a number of successful BMX riders moving across to the MTB world, which is something we'd never have dreamed of happening a couple of years ago.

With its newfound credibility MTB dirt-jumping has firmly established itself as an important part of MTBing that will be around for a long time yet.

Although many of the techniques that dirt-jumpers use are based around impressive tricks, every MTB rider will at some point find themselves catching some air, whether they intend to or not! So even if you're a diehard cross-country rider some of the fundamental dirt skills will be very useful riding tools to have.

24: Basic Jump Technique

It wouldn't really be much use starting off learning to jump without getting the fundamental technique out of the way first. Beginners should try and find a medium-sized tabletop jump like the one in the pictures. Most BMX tracks will have something similar, or if not you can build a small tabletop-style jump (ie flat on top). It's not a good idea to take this or any of the techniques we'll be going over on to double jumps until you're really comfortable in the air.

Before you even attempt to get off the ground, roll over the jump a few times until you feel relaxed enough to hit the jump faster. The most important thing is to stay relaxed and loose on the bike so that you can react to how the bike responds to the jump. Hitting the jump stiff is one sure-fire way to hurt yourself. Stay calm and control the bike rather than just being a passenger.

1 Approach the jump at fast jogging speed, keeping your eyes on the lip of the jump. At around 10–12ft (3–3.5m) from the lip compress your arms and legs and move your weight back on the bike.

2 As you roll up the transition, move your weight a little further back. As the front wheel leaves the lip pull back on the bars, helping to loft the front wheel.

3 The next part happens fast so you'll need to be quick. The back wheel will naturally get kicked into the air by the lip but your front wheel will be much higher than the rear. Flatten the bike out by moving your weight forward a little and allowing the rear wheel to level out by sucking it up with your legs.

4 To land smoothly, re-extend your legs so that they're virtually straight, which means you've got plenty of natural suspension to soak up the landing. As you get more confident and proficient you can drop the nose of the bike into the landing for an even smoother touchdown.

88

25: X-up

The good news is that the X-up isn't a hard trick to learn at all. The bad news is that it's a very hard trick to learn well and to make look natural. Let's make no bones about it – a bad X-up looks revolting. Either a non-committed half-baked attempt or, worse still, a bandy-legged effort with your knees poking out won't just get you zero style points, it may well get you laughed out of the skatepark or trails.

There's a couple of things you need to consider before setting out to learn the X. First off, figure out which way feels most natural for you to turn the bars. The majority of riders find it easier to lead with their stronger arm (the one you write with etc) but there's no hard and fast rules to this – just try both ways and see which one works for you.

Secondly, your bike and its set-up has quite a bit of influence over how you X-up. Somewhat ironically the trend for short jump frames has caused havoc if you happen to have large feet – the front wheel clips your foot on maximum extension and can be dangerous too. Check this isn't a problem before you hit the jumps by turning the bars all the way round whilst leaning against a wall. Also consider trimming your bars down a bit, which makes it much easier to get the bars round. Lastly, check your fork crown doesn't foul the downtube of your frame. This used to be a bigger problem than it is now, but certain frame and fork combinations can still cause an issue.

As always, start off slowly on a jumpbox or tabletop, twist the bars a little bit at a time until you can turn them a full 180° or further.

4

1 Approach the jump at fast jogging speed and set yourself up as you would for a regular jump. As you near the lip compress your arms and legs and move your weight back on the bike.

2 As the front wheel leaves the lip pull back on the bars and allow the transition to kick you into the air. Once the rear wheel is off the ground, shift your legs a little towards the back of the bike, and lock your knees against the nose of the saddle to prevent the bars from clipping your leg and that horrible knees-out style.

3 With your knees tucked out of the way start to twist the bars around as far as you can before you feel the bike begin to drop. Keep the movement smooth, don't snatch at the bars and get out of shape in the air. The movement needs to be like a reflex action crossing and uncrossing the bars, but hold the **X** as long as you can.

4 When you feel the bike start to drop, immediately uncross the bars, again keeping the motion as smooth as you can. Your arms should naturally stop themselves once you get them back to a straight position. Shift your weight forward so that it's more centred over the bike and relax your legs to soak up the landing.

step
1

26: Suicide Jump

The suicide jump can look amazing if you get it right. If you don't commit, or rush the jump, it will look shadier than the IKEA lighting department. Even advanced riders avoid this trick as it can be a nasty one to screw up (hence the name), but if you're confident in your riding and start small it's a great trick to add to your CV. What a lot of beginner riders don't realise is that getting this trick sorted has a lot to do with setting your bike up right. Saddle position and choice of saddle can play a massive part in getting suicides dialled. As always, practise on a jumpbox or tabletop before taking the trick to the trails.

1 Hit the jump fast – you'll need some decent height so that you can stretch the suicide as far as possible. Average running speed is about right. Make sure you have the trick locked in your head as you approach the lip.

2 As you leave the lip of the jump, make sure the bike is stable (not leaning to one side at all), pinch your knees together against the saddle, let go of the bars and physically throw your arms behind your body with quite a lot of force.

3 If you've timed the jump well you should hit the peak at almost exactly the same time as your arms reach full extension behind you. For a textbook suicide let the front wheel drop lower than the rear.

4 As your arms reach full stretch, hold for a second and then allow your natural reflexes to snap them back in front of you. Grab hold of the bars, release your grip on the saddle, transfer your weight back to the centre of the bike and pump into the landing.

step **2**

step **3**

step **4**

27: Tailwhip

1 You need plenty of height for the whip so hit the transition hard and fast and pump for as much pop out of the lip as you can. Again, try to visualise the trick in your head and be confident that you'll pull the jump. If you don't commit you'll be eating dirt or ply before you know it.

2 As you leave the lip, get off the rear of the bike and give the back end a big boot with your back foot. You can do this from the pedal or just give the seat-stay and tyre a big helping of your size ten.

3 As the back end starts spinning, you need to give it a helping hand by using your shoulders to propel the frame around. The action is like a circular whipping motion, which will help the back of the bike on its way.

Standard MTBs aren't really that well suited to tricks like tailwhips, with miles of gear and brake cable to contend with. Saying that, though, the first tailwhip we saw on an MTB was Kirt Voreis on a fully loaded Haro downhill bike – so if that's what floats your boat then it shows that it can be done.

On a single-speed, one-braked dirt bike there are still hassles involved, but tailwhips have definitely arrived in MTB dirt-jumping and what was once rarer than an honest politician is now a must-have trick for any serious contender.

Tailwhips look amazing, and of all the big contest tricks the whip gets big respect from riders because as well as being one of the most risky it's also one of the most technical.

Learning tailwhips is a messy old business and a lot of riders will try to find a foam pit or lake to try them out in first before hitting a jumpbox or tabletop. The biggest hurdle is getting the bike all the way around. Most riders will clatter themselves a few times after only kicking the frame halfway around. If that hasn't put you off, the whip is one of the most spectacular variations you can pull on an MTB, so if you've reached a level where you feel confident enough to try them, go for it.

TIP: You may want to run a zero compression cable like an Odyssey Slic Kable or Gyro if you get into tailwhips and barspins in a big way.

④ Keep your back foot high so that the frame doesn't clip your leg as it completes the spin. Aim to plant your front foot on the pedal as soon as the frame comes around. You might find it easier to catch the bike by landing with your foot on the seat-tube/top-tube junction whilst you're learning. Once you have your front foot safely on the pedal/ top-tube you're virtually there. Get your back foot to the pedal and ride away.

28: 360

The 360 is still one of the most impressive tricks you can pull on an MTB. Getting it wrong can be pretty hard on you and your bike. And the thing is, you *will* get quite a few wrong before you get them wired. Bailing from a 360 is one of the weirdest experiences you can have on a bike. Disorientation doesn't even come close to describing it – you have virtually no idea where you are, so you can't prepare for the old tuck 'n' roll and hope to get up with a scrap of dignity left. Even with 24in wheels an MTB is a lot longer than a BMX, which makes it that much harder to rotate. Riders who pull them on 26-inchers deserve some kind of medal.

I'm not doing a great job of selling them so far am I? OK, they're hard and they can hurt, and they can break you and your bike, but ask any of the very few riders who can pull them consistently what their favourite trick to do is and most of them will say the 360.

This trick is definitely one for the tabletop or jumpbox before you take it to the trails. When you're learning 360s you end up worrying so much about getting the bike around that you don't travel any distance over the jump; so you need to be really happy with the rotation before moving them on to a double jump. Once you get really good, go for super stylish 360s with the bike in a nosedive all the way around.

step 1

step 2

step 3

1 You don't need masses of speed for learning the 360. Aim to hit the jump at a fast jogging speed. As you approach the transition you need to start carving in the direction you want to spin.

2 Even before you've left the lip, keep carving hard in the direction of your turn. Aim to be starting your rotation before you've even left the transition of the ramp. Keep your hips locked parallel to the frame and twist hard with your upper body.

3 As the bike leaves the lip, allow your upper body to lead it. Keeping your hips locked will allow this to happen. Looking over your shoulder in the direction you're turning serves two purposes. It encourages your body to twist in that direction and also helps you to spot the landing once you're round.

4 When you're almost around you should be able to spot the landing. Straighten up by letting your torso uncoil itself. Your head should be almost facing forwards by now too. Cover your rear brake in case you don't make it all the way and aim to get the front wheel down first for a smooth landing.

360

step
4

step
1

step
2

step
3

step
4

29: Barspin

Barspins are relatively new to MTB dirt and park riding. The trick went mainstream in BMX about 15 years back, but it's taken until a couple of years ago for MTB riders to take it on. But as always happens, once a few riders start pulling them the psychological hurdle is out of the way and the trick now features in most top riders' KOD runs (an internal jam-style contest where the best rider is crowned King).

There's plenty to go wrong in a barspin, as anyone who's got one wrong will tell you (I have the scars to prove it), but without doubt they're still one of the most technical and slick-looking jumps you can pull on a 24- or 26-incher.

From a bike set-up point of view there are a few things you need to sort out before you join the barspin club. The risk of clipping your foot on the front wheel and preventing the wheel from spinning is the biggest and most dangerous barrier to getting the trick nailed. If your front wheel can't spin freely all the way around without clipping your shoe then you may as well give up now. Also, cables are a big issue. If you run gears you'll need to get rid of them. It is possible to run longer gear cables, but the extra resistance from a gear cable coiling around the headtube can cause problems. If you run a front brake, get yourself a hollow star-fangled nut from any good BMX shop and feed the cable through your fork steerer. For back brakes run a long outer cable, preferably something with low compression like Odyssey linear cables, which don't affect your braking once the bars are rotated. Or if you get into barspin tricks in a big way, install a gyro. A lot of riders complain about getting these things set up right, but usually they don't understand how they work. A well-set-up gyro will work as well as any regular brake cable. I recommend the Snafu Mobeus gyro, as it seems to pull a little more cable and has loads of adjustability.

Practise as much as you can on the flat by popping the front wheel up and experimenting with the speed of the spin and catching the bars again.

1 You need plenty of height for barspins to buy yourself as much time as possible, so hit the jump fast and make sure you get plenty of pop out of the transition.

2 Barspins happen really fast so as soon as you're clear of the take-off, move your legs back and lock your knees around the nose of your seat. You need your knees well out of the way or things will certainly end in tears.

3 Now the fun part. With your knees stabilising the bike and preventing you from falling off the back, throw the bars as smoothly as you can. From your earlier practice you should know exactly how hard you need to throw to get them round.

4 The opposite hand to the one you throw the bars with should be ready and waiting for the catch. When the bars get to about 270° round, all being well they'll meet up with your waiting hand. Use the catching hand to straighten the bars up, replace your other hand and get ready for landing.

Street & Park

Street & Park & Skills Park

Almost as an extension of the dirt-jumping scene, MTB riders have recently become a regular sight at indoor and outdoor skateparks all over the world. Likewise the street-riding phenomenon has grown enormously over the last couple of years and riders are testing their skills on man-made obstacles like walls, ledges and steps. Again the MTB proves its versatility by taking to street-based riding with ease. The small bombproof dirt-style frames that were designed to handle big jumps also took to the concrete amazingly well. You can even buy street-specific frames and products now for riders who need features like grind-plates and the ability to run pegs. Skatepark and street-riding can cross over, with many street obstacles like ledges and banks being mimicked in plywood and built to be abused.

And of course indoor skateparks are a lot more reliable when the weather isn't so great. If you can't get out and ride, there's usually a skatepark nearby where you can practise your dirt-jumping techniques without getting soaked or frozen!

Many street skills can cross over to your off-road riding – riding cambers, drops and steps have obvious parallels out on the trails – and any time spent riding is inevitably going to improve your skills.

30: Riding Stairs

Riding down steps is a pretty basic skill for any wannabe street rider and will help lead on to some much bigger and more impressive moves later on. From a technical point of view it's a really easy thing to master, but when you start out you may find it a little daunting. If you think about it, though, riding steps is just like riding down a steep slope – just a little bumpier. The only thing you really need to be concerned about is controlling your speed. If you have a clear run out of the bottom of the steps then you can hit them pretty fast. If you don't, then you need to do some careful braking to keep things under control. The good thing is that you don't have to hit the steepest, longest set you find on your first day out. There are plenty of short sets out there with nice shallow steps for getting the hang of it.

1 Approach the steps at a slow but controlled speed. As you near the edge take your last opportunity to check for any pedestrians using the steps.

2 When you know you have a clear run, shift your weight back a little (how far will depend on the steepness of the steps), cover your rear brake and allow the front wheel to drop into the stair. Bend your elbows and knees so you can absorb the bumps from the steps.

3 When both wheels are on the steps, keep your speed in check by dragging the brakes a little. Try to avoid using too much front brake as this can force your weight forward. Keep enough momentum to hold your balance, but don't just let rip until you're really comfortable.

4 As you near the end of the stairs have another check for people or other obstacles. Once the coast is clear, get off the brakes and aim to get the front wheel up a little to make your exit as smooth as silk.

31: Ledge Drop

Ledge Drop

Dropping off a ledge is one of those vanilla moves that every street rider will at some stage need to master. Sure, on its own it can look pretty dull, but you still get quite a rush as you work up to dropping off higher ledges as you gain more confidence. You need to have this technique totally dialled to make any kind of progression as a street rider. Keep practising until it's innate. That way, not only will you be able to throw all kinds of neat little variations into the mix, but you'll also find you'll be able to get yourself out of all kinds of nasty situations by dropping off something or pulling out of an otherwise disastrous scenario.

Naturally, start off low – even a kerb will give you some idea of where to begin. Ideally start on something a little bit higher so you can get used to landing rear wheel first (a kerb may be a little low for this). Something around a foot off the ground is a good place to start off – if you mess it up, you'll get away with it, but it's high enough to get to grips with making sure the back wheel touches down first.

step 2

step 3

step 4

1 Ride up to the drop at quite slow jogging speed. You need to get into the habit of using good technique instead of momentum to get you off the drop safely. It's easy to just fly off and see what happens, but you'll have very little control over the outcome.

2 As the front wheel approaches the lip, compress your arms ready to pump off the drop. If you have front suspension you can use this compression to load the forks, which can give you a more predictable pop when you lift the wheel and makes sure you have their full travel at your disposal when you land.

3 Transfer your weight backwards and pop the front wheel off the ground. Aim to get it around 6in higher than the rear. Any higher and you risk flipping off the back when you land. Cover your back brake just in case.

4 When the bike is in freefall, straighten up your limbs so that you have plenty of natural damping left when you touch down. Keep the front end up and your weight still over the back. Compress as you land and transfer your weight forward to prevent looping out.

Ledge Drop 105

step 1

step 2

32: Wall Ride

Wall rides look amazing and feel just as good too, but they take quite a bit of practice and bottle to learn. Don't be put off, though – they're not as hard as people tend to think. The main hurdle is getting your head around riding along a vertical wall. It's easy to panic and freak out, which usually leaves you sliding back down the wall or ploughing straight into it. If you think about those walls of death they have in circuses, you see guys on motorbikes riding walls like they're flat. The basic principle is kinda similar but obviously you don't have an engine to keep the momentum going.

It's rare to find a wall with a suitable bank or kicker to help get you on to the wall, so I improvise with planks and bricks and recently have got hold of a basic plastic kicker I keep in the car. It's possible to wall-ride from a straight bunnyhop but we'll leave that one for the experts for now.

step
3

1 You need to hit the wall at a good speed to get any kind of distance. Hitting the wall kills a lot of your speed so if you go too slow you'll probably drop off.

2 Spot the area you want to hit on the wall as you approach the ramp. Take a wide line into the bank or kicker and carve across its transition.

3 Aim to hit the wall at about 45° to the ground with both wheels at the same time. Any steeper and you won't get the distance. Much shallower and you'll get no height whatsoever. Drop your inside shoulder a little to get the bike a bit flatter.

4 As you hit the wall allow the bike to roll smoothly. If you brake, the bike will try and straighten itself and you'll drop. When you feel the bike lose momentum get ready to pull out hard. Get the front wheel up nice and high and straighten up your arms and legs to absorb the landing.

step
1

step
2

33: Gap/Transfer

Most people wouldn't look at the space between two objects or pieces of land as anything more than exactly that. But to a street rider, any two lumps of solid stuff with a bit of distance between them suddenly becomes something else. It might seem weird to get excited about nothing, because that's basically what a gap is … but when you set your mind to getting across it on your bike, you'll soon figure out that nothing can be a lot of fun.

Riding gaps doesn't have to be just for maniacs either. A gap can constitute anything from a few inches to several metres. The idea is the same, and to a certain extent so is the technique. Obviously it should go without saying that you should start out with the small stuff before donning your best Evel Knievel suit and heading out to your local canyon. But once you get confident with judging your distance and speed, you'll soon be hunting out the biggest chunks of nothing you can find.

You can get away with quite a lot when you start out riding gaps. Flat-out speed and a blatant disregard for your own safety will get you across most things, but landing like a sack of spuds on the other side isn't too clever and you'll look a bit daft too.

1 **Make sure you've figured out your approach speed before you even consider starting (see tip below). Stay loose on the bike, and focus on your take-off point.**

2 **As you get near to the edge, compress your arms and legs ready to pop a big bunnyhop. A couple of inches before the edge pull back on the bars, transferring your weight backwards to get plenty of height out of the hop.**

3 **Just before the back wheel leaves the ledge, make the hop. Get as much pop as you can, allow the rear wheel to rise up and underneath you but aim to keep the front high.**

4 **Spot your landing and adjust your body position to suit. If you feel like you're going to come up short, aim to keep the front high. You'll probably get away with just a flat-spot on your rim and a bruised ego. If you're looking set for a clean landing, shift your weight forward a little but aim to come in rear wheel first for a smooth landing.**

step 4

step 3

Gap/Transfer 109

34: Stair Gaps

1 You need plenty of speed to clear the top set and the flat middle section so figure this out roughly using markings in a carpark for reference. After a while this will become second nature.

2 As the front wheel gets close to the edge of the top step pop your front wheel up. You won't be hopping as such, like you would on a regular gap, but just making a smallish pop to get you clear of the first few steps.

3 Stay relaxed on the bike, and keep your weight centred, with your elbows and knees bent to help soak up the landing. Keep an eye on the top of the bottom set of steps like you would a landing on a double jump.

4 Allow the front to drop so that you can try and match the angle of the steps with your bike. Just like trails riding, the closer you can get your bike to the angle of the downslope the smoother your landing will be. When you touch down on the steps get your weight back a bit, and pull up at the bottom to ride out cleanly.

step **2**

step **3**

step **4**

Stair gaps might seem a bit crazy, and they can take a pretty big toll on your bike and yourself if you get them wrong. That said, stair gaps are really good fun, but are definitely for the more experienced rider.

The idea is to find yourself a double set of steps with a flat section in the middle dividing them. You see these everywhere, particularly under subways (the things that go under roads – not the sandwich shops). The idea is to launch from the top, missing out the top set and middle section altogether to land on the bottom set. It sounds scary, but if you commit to the drop landing on a set of steps isn't as bad as you might think. The angle of the steps acts like a downslope and the speed you're travelling means you skim across the edges of the steps, so the bumps don't feel too harsh. You see a lot of guys doing step gaps on big travel freeride bikes, which will naturally make things smoother, but that doesn't mean that you can't ride them on a hardtail.

35: Tyre Tap

The tyre tap is predominantly a park or ramp trick but you might be lucky enough to find a naturally occurring street section that you could use instead. If you can find a ledge or bank leading on to a flat section, these are perfect for tyre taps. If you can't find anything, just about any skatepark will have a suitable ramp or bowl you can learn on.

The tyre tap is essentially where you pop out of the ramp or bank, turn the bike approximately

step
1

90° in the air, land on the back wheel and stall for a bit before dropping back in again.

Tyre taps are much harder than they look, but any street rider worth their salt should have them in their trick bag. Once you have them dialled there are countless tricks and variations you can add to the vanilla tyre tap. Also, if you ride a lot of park you'll be able to link up all kinds of lines into one fluid run by pulling a nice safe tyre tap between your big tricks.

1 For tyre taps you need to have your speed sorted or you'll be working extra hard to get them under control. Have a few runs at the ramp and work out how fast you need to be going to just pop cleanly out on to the deck.

2 Carve across the transition of the ramp a little to help send you in the right direction. Allow the front wheel to pop out of the coping and encourage the bike to turn by twisting with your torso.

3 As the rear wheel leaves the ramp continue to twist a little and allow the bike to become airborne courtesy of the ramp's natural transition. Lock the back brake and plant the rear wheel a couple of inches past the coping (the tubular edge to most ramps) or edge of the ramp.

4 Keep your weight back so the front wheel stays nice and high. Stall on the back wheel for as long as you can. When you feel the balance start to slip, make a big hop back into the ramp. You should only have to twist the bike another 45° to get cleanly back into the ramp's transition.

step **3**

step **2**

step **4**

Tyre Tap 113

Barspin Drop

36: Barspin Drop

As we've already seen in Skill 29, barspins haven't been around in mainstream MTBing for that long. All the cables we have to contend with tend to get in the way a bit. But with a bit of tinkering, either by spending a bit of time learning to set up a gyro properly or by using longer cables, you can barspin an MTB just as easily as any BMX. Barspins always look the business on dirt or street and one of the most fundamental variations of the barspin is to do it off some kind of ledge.

As with most of these scary-looking tricks, they look much harder than they actually are. The biggest thing for most riders to overcome is the fear of letting go of the bars. There are a few things you can do to make the process a little less daunting. Grab yourself a decent dirt saddle with a textured, wide back section. This makes gripping the seat with your knees a load easier. Also spend a couple of minutes sorting your seat height out. Stand up on the pedals and lean against a wall for support, then with your pedals level, set your seat so you can comfortably grip the nose between your knees. You'll probably find this is a little higher than you're used to, so maybe find a compromise you're happy with.

1 Approach the drop with enough speed to comfortably clear the ledge. Have a few regular runs to make sure you have this sorted. Now is definitely not the time to be dropping the front wheel.

2 Shift your legs back a little so they're clear of the bars as they rotate. Pinch the nose of your seat with your knees so that you don't slip off the back of the bike when you throw the bars.

3 Keep the front high as it leaves the edge of the drop. If you throw your bars clockwise, release your left hand and keep it waiting patiently for the bar to come back around. Spin the bars nice and fast and aim to catch them at around 270° through the spin with your waiting hand.

4 Once you've caught the grip, allow the bar to continue around so that it's pointing in the right direction again. Get your other hand back to the grip as quickly and smoothly as you can and prepare to soak up the landing. If you miss the bars altogether, let the bike drop and step off the back of it.

step 2

step 3

step 4

Barspin Drop

115

37: Handplant

You can probably count on one hand the number of MTB riders who can cleanly pull the handplant consistently. If you've never come across a handplant before, it's essentially the same trick you see skaters and rollerbladers pulling out of halfpipes, but on a bike. The main difference is that on a bike the rider uses the handplant to get over an obstacle (in this example a spine ramp) rather than popping one at the top of a ramp and dropping back in the same way, like a skater would. Bikes are just too big and clumsy for that, but a few riders in MTB and BMX have figured out how to pull them over spines, and some skateparks have a specific rail installed just for this kind of thing. A few US riders have even set up natural handplant obstacles with kickers, sending them over tree branches which they plant on and ride out. It looks crazy and has to be one of the most technical park tricks out there.

step 3

step 4

1 You need to find a decent spine ramp or volcano with good steep transitions so that you have plenty of clearance for the bike. A nice compact bike with 24in wheels is definitely an advantage for this trick.

2 As the front wheel leaves the lip, suck the bike up by compressing your legs and allowing the whole bike to come up underneath you. Get your weight bias across to the side you want to lay the bike over and throw the bike upwards using your momentum.

3 Get the hand you want to plant off the grip. It's probably easiest to use your strongest arm, as the combined weight of a bike and your body isn't exactly light. Grab a big handful of the coping or top of the ramp and tweak the bike out into a kind of tabletop by using your bodyweight and your forward momentum.

4 When the bike reaches the peak of the plant it will get light for a second before the balance slips and the bike starts to drop. As this happens, allow the bike to drop and push away from the ramp with the arm you're stalling on. Get your hand back to the grip and aim to twist the bike so that you're pointing as straight as possible down the landing.

Handplant 117

Downhill Skills

It could be argued that downhill is MTBing in its purest form. Certainly it's as close to MTBing's origins as you can get, but balloon-tyred beach cruisers have now been replaced by hardware with several inches of suspension travel, components that can withstand enormous speeds and forces, and braking systems that can slow a rider from speeds occasionally in excess of 60mph.

Downhill riders today are almost unrecognisable as the evolutionary conclusion of the 1970s pioneers that started mountain biking as we know it.

Every aspect of their kit has been honed to create bikes and machinery that can handle riding off-road at speed and also protect the riders should they experience the inevitable crash. Full-face helmets, full-fingered gloves, spinal protection, joint pads, goggles and reinforced clothing are all part of the modern downhillers' arsenal.

The bikes are now works of engineering genius, suspension systems that offer controllable, adjustable travel and damping and, of course, the hydraulic disc braking systems that can bring you to a halt from ludicrous speeds.

Professional downhillers are the big celebrities of the MTBing scene, often larger-than-life characters who travel the world riding down mountains that many of us would struggle to walk down. The standard of riding has reached a level that usually means that the winners' podium is generally only separated by fractions of a second. All mountain bikers get to experience the thrill of riding fast down hills, and the basics of downhilling are common to all types of mountain biking, but to take things to the next level and experience MTB downhilling in its truest form means you need to learn and become proficient in all of the following skills if you really want to fly.

38: Rocky Chutes

This kind of section is typical of many found on a proper UK downhill – not particularly long but fairly steep and peppered with rocks and ruts all vying to throw you off course. Not only that, but the exit can often throw up its own challenges too, so always ensure that you walk the section first to assess any dangers.

You'd be surprised what you can actually ride through, but even the smallest rocks and ruts can cause a few problems if you hit them awkwardly. By taking care on the entrance and dropping in as relaxed as possible you can help to make sure you get a clean run through.

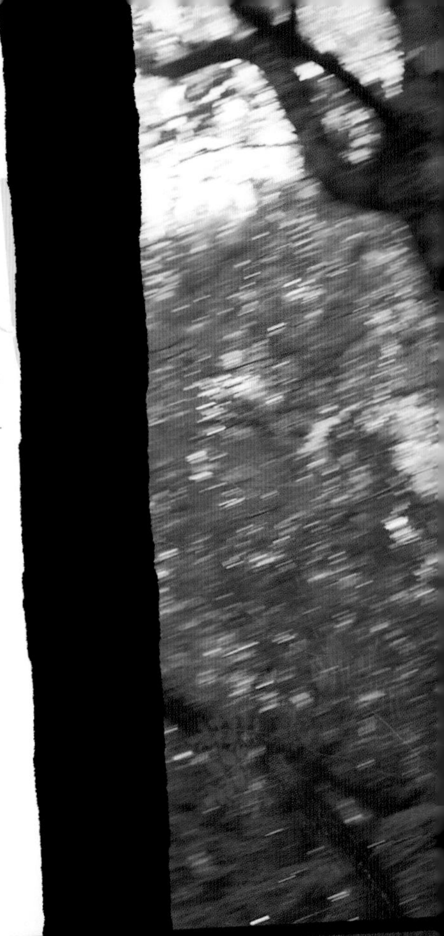

step 1

step 2

step 3

120

Rocky Chutes

step
4

1 As you approach the section, brake early, scrubbing your speed so that you enter the chute at a controlled speed.

2 As you drop into the chute, focus on the exit and choose your line through. Aim for the straightest line possible.

3 Keep your weight well back and try and avoid excessive use of the front brake. Allow the bike to move beneath you over the rocks – stay relaxed.

4 At the bottom of the chute keep focused on the next section and get back up to speed.

39: Obstacle Rocks

step 1

step 2

step 3

This kind of rock is more likely to be a feature of a World Cup event or Alpine mountain trail than your average UK downhill run, but other large obstacles can be tackled in a similar way to this. The most obvious advice is to check out the obstacle thoroughly beforehand. On most obstacles there will be an obvious line if one exists, so have a clamber over it on foot and examine the line in, over and away from the obstacle. If you can picture a reasonably straight line that gets you over the rock cleanly then that's where you need to go. It's not unheard of for pro riders to use markers to set themselves up for something like this – something like a twig or stone can be invaluable to help spot that line at speed.

This kind of obstacle takes a great deal of commitment to clean first go, so it's well worth taking a few attempts, building up to a complete run when you're comfortable. You can even ride up on to the top of the rock, regain your balance then drop back in.

step 4

1 Check the section out thoroughly and plan your line carefully. If the line is blind as on this rock use a distinct mark or shape as a reference point.

2 Approach the rock or obstacle at a decent speed so that you have enough momentum to carry you over it. Cover your brakes to make any emergency adjustments, but try to avoid scrubbing too much speed.

3 As you get on to the obstacle transfer your weight towards the rear of the bike. If you're carrying too much speed, dab your brakes (don't lock them) and prepare to ride the downside.

4 Once on the downside of the obstacle, as you reach the bottom pull the bars back hard to get the front wheel up. Try to get the bike into a manual to make the transition from rock to floor smoother. You can then accelerate away from the obstacle.

40: Large Rocks

Large Rocks

step
1

step
2

step
3

step
4

Large rocks can be a nightmare to ride – they're rarely uniform in size and shape and there's usually very little room for error. These rocks often punctuate a very fast section of trail and their sharp and angular non-uniform edges make them incredibly difficult to ride predictably and consistently. Often the best method to use with a section like this is to attempt to jump over them to avoid the problem altogether, but if this isn't an option then you need to develop a technique to handle such situations.

The best policy is to ensure that you don't carry too much speed into the section on your first few runs, as braking on uneven surfaces is unpredictable at best and occasionally dangerous at worst. Figure out the cleanest route through and aim to stick to that line.

1 If the approach is fast, scrub your speed as much as possible before you enter the section. Do all your braking before you get to the rocks.

2 Make sure you know your line and stick to it confidently. If you ride over the rocks, avoid braking on uneven surfaces and keep your weight back in case you catch your front wheel.

3 If you're riding around the rocks, keep your cranks level at the quarter-past-three position and watch out for edges that may clip your pedals.

4 Above all stay relaxed and let the bike move around beneath you.

Large Rocks

41: Roots

Roots are a common trail feature and are notoriously difficult to ride fast and cleanly.

Riding roots is all about total commitment and knowing the trail beforehand. You need to know the line through the section intimately – you won't be able to see what's going on ahead so to a certain extent you'll be riding from memory. The better you know the line and what comes after it, the faster you'll be able to hit the section.

step 1

step 2

step 3

step 4

1. Ensure you know your line precisely before attempting a run.

2. If the run into the section is rocky or rooty, try to skim the top by unweighting the bike. This way when you get to the roots you'll be more composed.

3. As you enter the section, stay light on the bike so that it can move as it hits the roots. Use flat sections between the roots as braking surfaces to control speed. Avoid braking on wet roots.

4. As soon as the section is cleared, get back on the gas.

step
1

step
2

42: Fade Drop

1 Always check the exit for hazards or obstacles before attempting to ride a fade drop. Clear any loose rocks or obstacles as you'll be hitting this type of jump blind so you need to be sure the trail is clear.

2 Hit the drop slowly to begin with, placing the bike quite high on the downslope until you build confidence and can drop faster and further. Pre-jump the drop so you can stay as close to the ground as possible.

3 Aim to match the angle of the downslope as closely as possible with your wheels so the transition into the landing is as smooth as possible. Stay low on the bike with your weight behind the seat and get prepared for the impact when you put the wheels down.

4 Absorb the landing with your arms and legs, but keep your weight well back so the impact doesn't force you over the bars.

step 3

The fade drop often catches riders out. The trail suddenly drops away and if you don't control it you're left dangling a few feet in the air with a nice crash to look forward to. There are a couple of techniques for dealing with the fade. You can either scrub all your speed and roll off the edge (safe, but very, very dull) or you can attack the fade and actually get more speed out of it. The second method is obviously the faster technique, but only if the line into the drop is clear and smooth and there are no obstructions to worry about.

Always have a few slow runs at the drop, getting used to riding the down-slope of the fade and to the sudden pickup in speed as gravity takes over. Pro riders will pre-jump into the drop from a vast distance away from the edge, landing smoothly in the down-slope, using their momentum to squeeze every ounce of speed out of the section.

step 4

Fade Drop

43: Speed Jump

**step
1**

**step
2**

The speed jump can save a racer valuable seconds on a very tight course. It also lets you control the bike over a section of trail that may kick you up when you need to be on the ground. Once again there are two ways of dealing with this kind of obstacle. The first is to allow the bike to take off, but keep it very low – useful if the ground is very uneven. The second is to completely absorb the jump and ride over the top of it.

The best kind of jump to practise the technique on is a nice long and low tabletop – the kind you'll find at any BMX track worth its salt. These jumps will kick the bike quite high off the ground unless you take measures to prevent that from happening.

Try to have a couple of normal runs at the tabletop to get a feel for how the transition spits the bike into the air. Familiarise yourself with this feeling of being 'popped' so that when you come to attempt to speed jump the tabletop you'll have a good idea what you need to counteract.

step 3

step 4

1 **Approach the jump as fast as you feel comfortable. If the run-in is very fast scrub some speed on your first few attempts.**

2 **As your wheels touch the transition of the jump, do a small bunnyhop before you get to the lip.**

3 **Keep the bike low by absorbing the kick from the take-off by staying low on the bike and absorbing the upwards momentum with your arms and legs.**

4 **Having avoided the main kick of the jump by doing this, now plant your rear wheel hard on top of the jump by physically forcing it down with your legs. Get pedalling as soon as you can and you'll hardly lose any speed at all.**

131

Speed Jump

step
1

step
2

44: Steep Drops

Short drops around a couple of feet high can be hard to know how to ride. Most of them are much easier to just launch off and get on with it, but occasionally the landing won't allow this and you'll have to just ride it out. This can be more daunting than launching off it, as you'll most probably be riding down a couple of feet of vertical trail. With a section like this the priority is getting through in one piece, so speed isn't so much of an issue.

Sections like this crop up a lot on race courses, being great for spectators as there's always plenty of variety in how riders take them on. It's always best to have the confidence to just ride through them, though, as was mentioned above, conditions don't always allow you to simply launch over the whole thing, and sometimes the tactical line into the following section makes it faster to ride through in a controlled state than risk getting a difficult jump wrong.

step
4

step
3

1 Always check the run out of the drop and get some idea of your line through the section.

2 Scrub as much speed as you can on entry. Focus on the exit and where you want the bike to go. Get your weight back as far as possible, extend your arms and get behind the saddle.

3 Avoid locking your brakes; instead aim to feather them to control your speed. A locked wheel is not as easy to control as a rolling one.

4 Pull up on the bars hard to get the front wheel up before the bottom. This will help prevent you from disappearing over the bars.

45: Berms

A berm is simply the term used for a heavily banked turn. Either naturally formed or man-made, berms help you get round a corner as fast as possible (imagine a velodrome or IndyCar circuit).

However, berms can be pretty daunting to ride. It takes quite a bit of faith to believe that the cambered corner will hold you in so that you can ride it flat out. Most new riders are pretty wary of hitting berms fast, but the irony is that the faster you hit them, the safer they are. The most common mistake made is braking inside the berm and not focusing on the exit of the turn. If you brake inside a berm the bike is forced upright and you lose your line, often popping out of the top of the berm. Likewise if you're concentrating on what your front wheel is doing rather than looking ahead to where you want to go you'll fall off your line easily. To ride berms fast try the following:

1. **Brake before the berm and scrub enough speed to be comfortable in the turn.**

2. **Take a wide line into the berm to create a smoother curve. Don't brake inside the berm at all. If you do you'll pop out of the top.**

3. **Avoid using your bars to turn as much as possible. Use body English and trust the berm and your tyres to get you round.**

4. **Keep looking at the exit out of the berm rather than where your front wheel is and you'll stick to your line.**

step 1

step 2

step 3

step 4

Berms 135

46: Fast Corners

Fast corners are where a lot of time can be won and lost on a race run. The speed in which you can comfortably get round a corner is a delicate mixture of conditions, tyre choice, technique and confidence. On a downhill course, flat-out bends are where you really get to see a good rider shine. They know their line and have a very good idea how their bike will react to the surface of the corner. The finite changes during the bend are all reactive and will come with time and practice. A shift of weight or a dab of the brake can make the difference between staying upright or climbing out of the bushes.

Many of the pros use a technique called 'riding light' when cornering on fast bumpy turns. Using a similar technique to a bunnyhop but without actually letting the wheels leave the ground, you unload the suspension, the bike stays light and skims the top of rocks, roots or any other obstacle. This means your tyres stay hooked into the dirt so that you can carry speed without losing traction.

step 1

step 2

step 3

Fast Corners

1 If the corner is long and not too sharp you can afford to brake quite late, even slightly into the turn itself; just avoid locking up. On tighter fast bends avoid doing any braking at all in the turn.

2 Take a wide line into the bend to make the turn less sharp. Keep looking at the exit of the turn to hold your line.

3 Try and pick the smoothest line through the bend. Avoid any sharp movements or changes in direction.

4 On rocks or roots use the 'riding light' technique described above to skim over the obstacle.

47: Technical Corners

Downhill isn't always about flat-out speed. Some courses are more demanding technically and require a bit more of a light touch. Cambers, roots, rocks and gulleys all add technical issues when trying to get down the hill as quickly as possible. In situations like this, your brain is your best ally. Think quickly and develop strategies that allow you to cope with whatever the hill throws at you.

Speed is often not your friend in these situations, so aim to enter the section at a speed you know you have maximum control at for the situation. There's far less margin for error when the trail is that much more technical. If the hill is cambered and slippery ensure that your tyre edges are biting by loading that side of the bike with your bodyweight. If the hill has rocks or roots then use them to your advantage – obstacles like these are perfect for using to block a slide, or you can actually ricochet off them on to a better line, like a lot of pro downhillers do.

1 Enter the section in full control, scrubbing as much speed as possible before you get there.

2 Lock the rear wheel, staying relaxed and centred on the bike. A bit of opposite lock on the bars will make the slide more controllable (imagine motorbike speedway).

3 Use your hips to direct the slide until the bike is set up to exit the corner.

4 Straighten the bars up and get the power down out of the bend.

step 4

step 3

139

Technical Corners

step
1

140

Sweeping Bends

48: Sweeping Bends

Sweeping bends are tighter bends that change the direction of the course quite dramatically in a short space. You'll sometimes see these linked together on a course, traversing the hill; these are known as switchbacks. As the name suggests, the best technique is to ride them in a smooth sweeping motion – which is not quite so easy when you throw rocks and roots into the equation. The watchword here is flow. You need to stay relaxed and loose whilst being able to shift your entire bodyweight across opposite sides of the trail at a second's notice. The technique is almost like a less frantic version of slalom technique, where you see the bike literally being thrown into the turns.

1. Always have a few practice runs and choose the best/fastest lines by experimenting with the alternatives.

2. Try to maintain speed but remain safe – it's always faster to stay on the bike than be recovering from a mistimed switchback.

3. Using the unweighting technique described earlier, deal with the rocks, drop your inside shoulder into the turn and stay off the brakes.

4. Keep looking out of the bend to hold your line. Try to remember to knock the gears down a notch so that you can accelerate out of the bend.

step 3

step 2

step 4

The discipline of 4X has evolved from a number of sports to become one of the most spectacular and exciting types of competitive MTB riding there is. Even from MTB's early days, riders used to race head to head on two separate but matching tracks in a traditional ski-style slalom event called dual slalom.

The courses were often steep and reasonably challenging, with plenty of potential for crashes. BMX riders were particularly adept at slalom racing and a lot of the early heroes were riders who had made the temporary switch to larger wheels.

However, over time as riders became more skilful and bikes improved the format started to look a little dated; also riders and spectators were getting annoyed that one small mistake at the top of the hill could mean that your entire run could be ruined.

Taking cues from BMX racing, 4X was born. Four riders raced together over a technical, downhill course. Tactics became far more important and with the riders racing at full speed only inches apart from each other over big jumps and round bermed turns, the spectators were once again given the exciting racing they craved.

4X riders are exceptionally skilled, and their bike handling is phenomenal. The speed and agility required to compete is incredible – not to mention the instinct needed to spot passing opportunities and the commitment to attempting overtaking moves, whether through a tight turn or by launching straight over another rider.

49: Gate Starts

Passing on a dual course is never easy. If you get a good gate start you stand a much better chance of keeping a lead as long as nothing goes wrong further down the hill. The gate start used in dual is identical to that used in BMX. A hinged metal gate is brought up in front of the front wheel and on the starter's command the gate drops and the riders sprint away. This is known as 'snapping'. The faster snap you get and the quicker you get out of the gate, the more chance there is of being well on your way to a win.

It takes a lot of practice to get out of the gate cleanly and as fast as you can. You can practise gates by propping a plank up and getting a friend to drop it for you. To get a good position on the bike – one in which you can get as much power to the back wheel as possible – try wedging the rear wheel against something solid so that you can experiment with your position until you find something that works for you. Many local BMX clubs have a gate practice during the week – ask if you can join them and you may even pick up some tips.

step 1

step 2

step 3

step 4

1 Establish a good position on the bike. Balanced and with the pedals level.

2 Ensure you've chosen an appropriate gearing (not too low, not too high) and that the gear is properly engaged.

3 Pick a spot and head for it. Let the other riders go round you if they have to.

4 Concentrate only on the starter's voice, don't get distracted. As soon as you hear the start command and the sound of the gate dropping, get on to the gas fast.

step
1

step
2

50: Doubles

Dual courses are peppered with jumps. Some courses provide chicken runs on some of the larger doubles, but if you want to race fast you'll need to know how to deal with most types of double jump. Whether the double is a small roller that you can ride through if you choose, or a massive set with a 40ft (12m) gap, you need to be able to ride all of them and everything in between. And fast.

Jumping doubles on a 4X course is more about confidence and speed than much else. Race jumps aren't designed to send you particularly high in the air, and the transitions tend to be more mellow with nice big landings. This means your jumping technique doesn't need to be the most stylish or beautifully executed example on the track. As long as you can confidently control the bike in the air and handle the landing, that's all you need to get started.

A BMX track is the best place for learning how to ride doubles. Most tracks will have a variety of sets that will allow you to develop the skills you need to take to the 4x or dual track.

step 4

1 You should have a good feeling of how much speed you need to clear a set of doubles before attempting to ride them. Practise on a tabletop jump and experiment with different speeds until you have a good feel for the speed you need to clear certain distances.

2 Hit the take-off with confidence and stay loose on the bike, allowing the transition to push you skywards. Aim to spot the landing as soon as you can, and try to flatten the bike out a little in the air. It's not a bad thing to keep your front end high at first so if you happen to case (come up short) the landing you should be able to ride out.

3 Midway through the jump, be aware of how far off the landing is and prepare to drop the nose of the bike as you approach the landing by moving your bodyweight forwards.

4 As you come in to land, aim to match the angle of the downslope as closely as possible by pumping the front end into the landing. As you get more confident and develop a good feel for riding jumps you can use this momentum to accelerate out of the double just by pumping.

step 3

51: Picking Racing Lines

Dual slalom requires very quick decision-making and lightning reflexes. A moment's hesitation could cost the race. A dual course is littered with jumps and turns but berms are one course feature that you can really use to your advantage if you know how to pick lines. A bermed corner is built up into a curved bank that allows you to corner much more sharply than you would on flat ground. It takes a little bit of faith to hit a berm flat out and expect it to hold you in. Beginners are prone to two main errors – looking in the berm at the front wheel and trailing a leg like a speedway rider. Looking at your wheel won't do you any favours, keep looking ahead at where you want to go rather than where you are going. It can be tempting to put a leg out too; it may feel safer but you'll throw your weight out and you won't get around the berm so smoothly.

It's a good racing tactic to stay close to the rider in front and pressure them into making mistakes by choosing a faster line and catching them off guard. If you spot a rider in front taking a low line on the berm, you can take the higher line and beat them to the exit by dropping sharply out of the berm and accelerating past them. Conversely if they took a high line, sneak through on the inside, hold your line firmly and you may cause them to make a mistake or lose speed. Always avoid braking in the berm itself. Braking forces the bike upright which will throw you off line and occasionally out of the berm. Always avoid braking in the berm itself. Braking forces the bike upright, which will throw you off line and occasionally out of the berm.

1 Stay close to the rider in front and watch which line they take.

2 React fast and spot the best line around or past them. Attack the gap.

3 Stay focused and hold your line with confidence until you are clear.

4 As soon as you're clear, get back on the gas and leave your competitor for dust.

step **4**

step **3**

149

Picking Racing Lines

52: Passing

Passing in dual is incredibly hard. The rider in front of you has the pick of lines and in 4x there may be three others doing their best to get past you. The techniques for passing are extremely loose and vary wildly from course to course. Some tracks may have a straight where you could simply outsprint a competitor. Some courses will favour a big jumper who has the bottle to take out other riders by going over the top of them. Other courses will be tight and you'll need to be watching like a hawk for slip-ups or gaps left by the rider in front.

It's no coincidence that a lot of the world's best dual and 4x riders are pretty well built. Technique will win you half the battle in a race, but you certainly can't be too delicate when it comes to beating the other rider or riders to the chequered flag.

The best riders out there are incredibly fit, skilful, and have a collection of tactics to ensure they have an exploit for every situation.

1 Watch for riders' weak sections and exploit them. Apply pressure and try to force an error.

2 If it's safe to do so, nail your opponent in a berm.

3 Practise big jumps and use the technique to pass riders overhead.

4 Don't be afraid of a bit of argy-bargy. Go in hard and you'll most likely come out better off. Think fast, use your gears well to get a good sprint in a clear section.

Trials Skills

MTB trials is yet another example of the versatility of the mountain bike. Trials have existed in various forms throughout the years, both on motorbikes and on bicycles. When trials riders discovered the MTB it was apparent that these small-framed, tough bikes with powerful brakes and grippy tyres were the perfect tool for riding bike trial courses. Hopping over gaps, dropping from ledges, ascending almost vertical trails and traversing rocks and logs were no problem for the MTB. The discipline became the ideal showcase for MTB bike-handling and trials demos soon became commonplace at bike events.

Riders don't need any special kit or equipment to ride trials on an MTB, which has helped to make the sport even more popular. Trials skills also cross over very well to general trail riding, and the skills required for trials can enhance your riding untold amounts. Traditional trials events take place on natural obstacles like rocks and logs but in recent years we've seen a lot of riders taking their skills to the streets, replacing natural obstacles with concrete, wood and steel. You can practise trials techniques almost anywhere, and obstacles are very easily improvised using whatever you can find.

Bunnyhops

53. Bunnyhops

The bunnyhop is a skill that all MTB riders should learn, and is also a fundamental technique for trials riding. The basic premise is to get both wheels off the ground without the need for a ramp or kicker, so you can get over obstacles like rocks and logs on the trail. The basic technique isn't very hard to learn – most riders can get the bike airborne after just a few hours. Building on that technique so that you can hop several inches at your discretion will enable you to apply the skill in a variety of situations and add a whole new dimension to your riding, allowing you to ride sections of trail that would have been impossible before.

For trials riding, bunnyhopping gives the rider the power to move the bike on and around obstacles that wouldn't be ordinarily rideable. To learn to bunnyhop, start by placing a small (movable) object like a drinks carton on the ground. Start slowly and build the object up in size as your technique develops.

step 3

step 4

1 Ride along at a steady jogging pace – you need a little bit of speed to help get enough distance to clear the object safely. Approach the obstacle standing up with your pedals level.

2 The rule of thumb for clearing an object is to start the hop at least the same distance away from the object as it is high. So if the object is a foot high, start the hop at least a foot before it. It can help to identify this spot by a chalk mark on the ground.

3 As you reach the take-off spot, throw your weight backwards and pull up hard on the bars to get the front wheel off the ground. Allow the wheel to come up as high as you need to comfortably clear the obstacle. Cover your rear brake in case you go too far – dabbing the brake will bring the front end back down.

4 With the front end clear of the object you need to get the back wheel up and over too. Throw the front of the bike forwards whilst simultaneously unweighting the rear by quickly moving your weight forwards again, dropping your heels a little and scooping the rear wheel up with your feet. Allow the rear wheel to come up beneath you by bending your knees. Once clear of the obstacle, absorb the landing using your elbows and knees to soak up the impact and ride away.

1 Using the backhop technique, set the bike up so that you're perpendicular to the object you're dropping from. You should now be facing the area you wish to drop to square-on.

2 Steady the bike and get your balance sorted. You may need to hop around on the spot for a bit until you feel comfortable.

3 Make small hops towards the very edge of the drop and prepare to make the pedal stroke to get you down. If there's any kind of gap involved, you'll obviously need to make it a larger stroke to get the distance. As you get right up to the edge allow the front to dip down a little, bringing it closer to the ground.

4 Put in the pedal stroke, releasing the rear brake as you do so. Reapply it as soon as you're clear of the wall to prevent looping off the back. Try to force the rear wheel down first; pulling the bars to your middle should ensure this. Absorb the landing and ride away.

156

Drops

54: Drops

One of the fundamental skills that trials riders need in their arsenal is the ability to tackle the drop-off. The backhop or pedal-kick works well for most drops and is the technique favoured by most riders.

The general idea is to move the bike around on the back wheel using small hops and jabs from the pedals to get forwards movement. To raise the front initially, put in a decent pedal stroke with your leading foot and catch the bike with the rear brake. Re-cock your pedals back to level, so that you can make another stab with them. Before the front drops, make a quarter pedal stroke with your leading foot, release the brake and put in a small hop. Re-cock the pedals. Again catch the bike with the rear brake. Repeat this motion as necessary – the more you load the rear brake with pedalling energy, the more explosive the hop can be. You need very effective brakes for this technique so spend some time ensuring that your brakes are working as best they can.

As always with any new technique, start small. You can actually learn this skill on the flat and move on to very small drops before working up to substantial drops once you have the technique mastered. Below is how to apply the backhop drop technique to a wall drop.

step 1

step 2

step 3

step 4

55: Getting On To An Obstacle

The obvious way to get up on to an obstacle is to use the straightforward bunnyhop. This is a very useful technique for anything up to about 3ft (0.9m) high, but larger obstacles require a slight twist to the variation. You may want to consider installing a bash-guard (a protective device that attaches to your cranks) for this technique to prevent damage to both your chainrings and the obstacle you're attempting to conquer. Avoid trying this technique on any obstacle that can be damaged easily. The technique below is known as a touch-hop and you'll use the motion generated by the 'touch' to be able to mount much higher obstacles than with a standard hop.

step 1

step 2

step 3

1 Approach the obstacle at a speed you're comfortable hopping a reasonable height at. It's best to start on something about 2ft (0.6m) high. A wall leading on to a flat top is perfect.

2 Pull up as you would for a standard hop, the difference being that you need to bump the front wheel on the edge of the wall. This makes the back end spring upwards as if you'd just pulled hard on the front brake. (This only needs to be a slight glance – any harder and you'll just bounce off the obstacle.)

3 As the wheel touches, throw the bike forwards through your legs and allow the back wheel to come up between them.

4 The rear wheel should now be up on the edge along with the front. On the first few attempts you'll probably come up a bit short. Grab hold of the brakes to stop yourself sliding backwards off the wall and put in a couple of forward hops to get both wheels on properly.

An Obstacle

step
4

160
Gaps

step
1

step
2

56: Gaps

In a traditional trail environment the best way to get over a really big gap is normally to hit it hard and launch over it. In trials, though, speed is not generally a priority and is limited on trials-specific bikes by the small chainring. Good technique has to replace brute force and a bit of finesse is called for. A very competent trials rider can traverse enormous gaps using a slightly modified technique to the backhop described earlier. The rear brake is used to store and then release forward momentum to help propel the rider across the gap.

step 3

step 4

1 Get on to your rear wheel using the backhop technique, and using small, controlled hops position yourself at the edge of the gap. Make sure you've established good solid balance before continuing any further.

2 Hold the brake a little as you begin to pedal-kick towards the edge. This loads up the stroke with more energy, which is released explosively as you release the brake.

3 As you make the final pedal stroke as you leave the edge, make sure you reapply the rear brake once the wheels are clear of the edge. Pull the bars up to your middle to ensure a rear-wheel landing.

4 To land the gap hop, make sure the rear brake is well locked on as your wheel touches down. Absorb the force of the landing by soaking the impact through your legs and arms. Find your balance and ride away.